You Brought Me Out

You brought me out to bring me into You.
Where I am today,
I can honestly say,
    that God, You alone brought me out
    to bring me in when I was deep in sin.

When I was stressed and possessed,
Lord, You brought me through my mess.

And this is my testimony,
    that I am still here today.
They didn't (or it didn't) take me out,
    they only (or it only) brought me closer
    to where you are.

I thank You, Lord, for bringing me through.

For Your wisdom now and forever more.
I thank You on this day for carrying me through.

There was a time in my life when I was afraid of the dark. I dreaded the night and hated when it was time to go to sleep. I was afraid to go to sleep because my mind was so consumed with spirits of anger, bitterness, suicide, hate, lust, and low self-esteem (just to name a few). Nighttime seemed to be when the demons of destruction were ready to take me under for good. There were many nights of me lying awake in agony and cursing God for putting me through my emotional trauma.

The nights were scary and seemingly never-ending. I prayed angrily to God one night to save me, to help me, to guide me. There were plenty of nights when I felt like God was not hearing my prayers. He never answered me back right then as I was crying and pouring my heart out to Him. He was ignoring me because I was a wretched sinner whom He wanted nothing to do with. The truth is that God was talking to me all along. I was too angry to hear what He was saying.

What He was telling me all along was that He hears me when I cry. He feels my pain when I am hurting and He loves me and He cares for me. The Bible says in Psalms 6:8, "The Lord has heard the voice of my weeping. The Lord has heard my supplication (petition); the Lord receives my prayer (NAS version)."

The good news is that God hears our prayers no matter what we are, who we are, or what we have done! He is always listening! Whether we pray when we are happy, sad, glad, or mad, He hears us. Thank God for that!

To the Woman of Purpose,

This book was written for you, the woman who has been drowned by darkness and is now eagerly seeking the marvelous light. I encourage you to look up to the sky where your help comes from. Look past the clouds in the sky and realize that there is a man up there looking down upon you who works behind the scenes on your behalf; so be of good cheer, and count your blessings and not your worries because God is greater than any situation or circumstance that you are facing right now.

Since you were called according to His purpose (Romans 8:28), everything you have been through has to work out for your good, because He says it in His word. God cannot and will not lie. God allowed all the trials, the hurt, and the pain to happen, so that one day, you would be transitioned and transformed into His likeness. God has plans for you to prosper; you have a future of hope and success regardless of where you are right now (Jeremiah 29:11).

My prayer for you is that before you turn this page and before you finish this book, you will seek God and know that you were born for a purpose and that you are here for a reason! I dare you to declare in your mind that you are a woman of purpose, because you are more than a conqueror!

I want you to know that I love you and that God loves you even more! I would like to hear from you, please feel free to contact me at WomanofPurpose2010@gmail.com.

Sincerely,
Hersha-Ann Smith

This book is dedicated to my children Kenisa and Isaiah. I am honored to be your mother and I thank God for the both of you every day. The plans that God has for you is greater than you and I can imagine. Always stand tall and remember to put God first in *everything* that you do. Always remember to practice having a relationship with Him instead of practicing religion. I love you both more than I can ever tell you in this lifetime.

To my sisters Lisa and Kendra you girls are my heart, I love you so much! I could not pick a better pair of siblings to share my life with because you are my best friends in the spiritual and the natural.

To our only brother Omar, we are glad to have you in our lives and we love you very much!

Acknowledgments

Thank you God for being head of my life and for giving me this great gift.

To my parents, thank you for molding me into who I am today. You both always encouraged me to shoot beyond the stars. Mom, I hope that I can continue to make you proud of me! Dad, you have to pay for your book, no free copy!

Special recognition to my grandmother who is a woman I will continue to model my spiritual walk after.

To my Uncle "Winky" I love you very much! Thank for your encouragement.

Shout out to my V1 crew on the USS WASP 2001-2004 Carpenter, Franco, Anol, David, Uncle Dirty, Todd, Alam, White, Murrel-Tanner, Flores, Riley, Caldiera, Haynes, Cordell, Parker, Senior Chief, Ferguson, Height, and the Fly 2 squad (Fly 2 always did the most work), love you all, you people will always have a place in heart! Friends forever!

To my Windsor High School c/o 2001 "Best Friends Forever" Katrina, Renee, Jaamal, Kylon, Ebony, and the rest you know who you are! I love you so much!

Thanks to Jet Photography for being my stylist, photographer, and sister for life!

Thank you Pastor Johnson and Spirit and Truth for planting me in my purpose! Thank you Women in Need for watering me in my walk!

Howard, Carter-Perry, and Taylor-Slaughter families have truly been blessings in my life! Love you all!

Thanks to E. Kirkwood for being a great friend and encouraging me through this process. S. Wilkerson, thanks for checking up on me when I disappeared! 4Life, we can make that movie and write that book when you're ready!

Thanks to my real friends and present family members for all your encouragement and well wishes you know who you are.

Over the Fence

What's a girl to do when she has to choose between God and man?

Chapter One

It's getting harder and harder to wake up in the morning for church. Today, it's just too cloudy, and I know it's cold outside. My hair won't do right. No matter how tight I put my ponytail, it just won't stay upright. I tried to pull my hair down and brush it to stay flat, but it became frizzy at the top. *I guess it's time for a perm now.* I frown at my reflection in the mirror. I'm not bad-looking. I have great skin, my almond-shaped eyes are quite sexy, and my nose is nice and round, not too big and not too small. I feel silly smiling at myself in the mirror. *My teeth could be a little whiter,* I think to myself. My makeup doesn't match what I want to wear. My striped brown suit doesn't seem to fit my body right. *Did I put on weight?* I ask myself. I do one of those side turns in the bathroom mirror and lift my shirt up to see what was going on under my clothes. I feel a little heavier. *Is that a roll forming at the side?* I look a little closer and decide to just run away from the mirror.

I just don't feel like anything is going right. *Snap out of it, Tami.* At this point, I know for sure I'm not going anywhere. I'll just watch church on television today. I need to stay home and clear my head about Chris. I just don't know how to feel about him sometimes. Sometimes I feel like I hate him, and then other times I feel like I'm in love with him. I think that maybe he's the reason why I'm feeling so sour about myself right now. The last time we spent time together, he looked at me so deeply, with this longing for me in his eyes. He even told me that I was beautiful and that I was "wifey material." *Is that the same thing as wife material? For some reason, that sounds a little different to me.* He makes me feel so good about myself, like I'm the most beautiful girl in the world.

We talked for hours about our lives and our dreams, and I really felt connected to him. He even kissed me good-night that night and said he would call me to come over. But I haven't heard from him since that day. Did I do something wrong? I mean, I told him that I wouldn't mess with him. There was no way I was going that far with him, at least not right now. I let him know I wasn't that kind of girl. Could that be why he hasn't called me yet? *I wonder if he is coming over today. I should give him a call.* Hopefully, he will pick up this time. It seems like the only time I get in touch with him is when he needs something. I have to be real with myself; the only reason why I'm not going to church today is because I don't want to miss the opportunity to spend time with him. *Church will always be there, right?* But then again, I'm always dropping the things that I want to do for this dude, and I don't think that he even does the same thing for me. Sometimes I feel so stupid for Chris. I feel like a little schoolgirl chasing a guy who doesn't want to be caught.

I keep calling, calling, and calling. There it goes again—that stupid feeling in my gut. I'll just have to ignore it. *I'll call him one more time and that's it. I promise.* I hate hearing his phone ringing. It is so annoying to just sit here like a dummy and hope that he will answer the phone. *Dang, he didn't answer the phone. Ugh, I'm so tired of him anyway.* I keep running back to him everytime. I don't know why I do that. Wait, no; I do know. I'm so drawn to him because he makes me feel beautiful and sensual at times. I also feel like I lose myself sometimes, like I always think more about him than I do myself. I have to get up and get dressed and get something to eat. I don't feel like doing anything today. Maybe I should go to church. But I really don't feel like going, besides, what if Chris comes over or something? No, maybe not. I know I have to do better. But I just can't and I don't know why.

I have to be real with myself. I would rather chill with Chris than go to church. I feel more of the desire for him than I do for church. I guess it is easier for me to sit here and wait on him than to go to church and hear a preacher. I'm going to watch it on television on one of those Christian channels. Doesn't that count? I don't want to force myself to go to church when I really don't feel like it! God knows my heart, and He also knows that I love Chris—of course, not more than I love Him, but at the same time, I can hold Chris and touch him. I don't really think I can do all that with a Bible. Ugh! That sounds so horrible, but that's how I feel. I have to be real. I still feel a pang of guilt though. I guess I will have to just make better decisions and stop being so hard on myself when I mess up. Oh, my phone is ringing. *Is it Chris?* It's restricted; I wonder who it is.

Chapter Two

I answer the phone (of course, expecting it to be Chris). I don't know if I exactly hid my disappointment when it wasn't him on the line.

"Hey Tami, are you coming to practice after service today?"

It was just Maxine, the choir director at church. She is also a good friend of mine. Suddenly, I feel myself getting just a little irritated. Why is she even calling me restricted? I'm trying to get my voice together before I talk to her. I didn't want to take my disappointment out on her.

"Yeah, I guess so," I answered, nonchalantly.

"So that means you're coming to church today?" Maxine asked. She sounded a little too excited. *Ugh, I don't feel like explaining myself today.*

"I don't know yet, I'm kind of not feeling too well. But I can make practice today, I think."

I feel bad about lying. God forgive me, but I simply don't feel like being bothered with church, singing, practice, or anything else. I just want to sit here at home and just chill. Gosh, why hasn't Chris called me yet? I can't wait to cuss him out and tell him about himself.

"Well, hopefully we will see you tonight. We miss you, girl." *Aww, that was nice of her. They miss me. I do have quite a voice in that choir. Well, I will just have to try to make it.*

"Okay well, I will try to make it for sure this time, Maxine. Thanks for calling."

I hang up the phone and turn the television to TBN. That's as close to church as I'm going to get today. *Why do I feel so lazy?* Who knows? The service on television is about knowing who you are and living your life out loud and not being ashamed to walk in Christ. I see that being a hassle for

people. *Especially for me.* It seems like I want to do right, but I just don't. Hmm, my spirit is willing but my flesh is so weak. Hey, I'm a sinner right? Who can cast a stone at me? I chuckle out loud at myself. Still no phone call from Chris. I'm just gonna call him again and he better answer. *I feel so stupid worrying about this dude, but who does he think he is?*

Oh, I need my Bible! I have to pick up where I left off in Psalms 6. I tried to dial his number again and still no answer. I have to make a promise to myself to not answer the phone if he calls and certainly not to call him, ever again. *I mean it this time, I really do.* If I text him, is it the same thing? *No, I won't do that either.* No phone calls, no texting. Nada. Nothing.

Whatever. I'm going to read my Bible now. That's the least I could do for missing church and not praying last night. I begin to read and I try to concentrate, but I can't. I have so much on my mind and I don't know what to do. I don't feel like praying either. I know that I should, but I don't feel like it. I close the Bible and I lay down on the bed. There is no way I can concentrate on reading or praying right now. *Lord, help me, please. I don't know what to do or why I feel the way I do. Please guide me. Ugh! I need help, like mental help! This can't be normal. God, please please please I can't get it out!* I can't even pray right now. That's odd, right? I used to love reading my Word. I couldn't sleep without a few verses or chapters. I still love the Word; it's just that right now it seems so dry and the chapters seem *so* long. I can't pray. I can't read my Word. I just can't…

Chapter Three

I must have fallen asleep during my temper tantrum because I woke up to my phone playing my favorite Alicia Keys song, "Unbreakable." I know it's Chris because I gave him that ring tone. A rushing wind of energy flows over me and I'm so happy and joyful. Yes! He called me back—sure, a few days and couple hours later, but at least he called me. I try to calm down to answer the phone. I don't want to sound *too* happy.

"Hello?"

"I thought you would be in church by now." He sounds so cute on the phone. His voice is deep and creamy. I love his Southern accent.

"Yeah, I was gonna go, but I didn't feel like it anymore." *Please ask me to come over,* I plead to myself with my fingers crossed. I wouldn't dare ask him to come over. He will have to suggest it. I really hoped that he would.

"I been calling your phone but you don't answer. Where you been?" I whined. Chris didn't answer right away. I wonder if I should have asked him that. I didn't want to tick him off or anything.

I start to worry. "Chris?" *Is he still on the phone or what?* Still no reply. Now my face is getting hot.

"Chris! Did you hear me?" He is still not responding to me.

"Hey, I have to call you back, okay?" he replied finally.

"Yeah, right—as if you really will call me back," I retorted.

"No, I really will call you later on. Whatchu doing later? You going back to church tonight?"

I am supposed to go to choir rehearsal, but if he is coming over, I know my plans will change—so I may as well change them now.

"No, I'm not going. Why, wassup?" *He wants to come over.* My spirit was lifting slowly with excitement. *Yay! He wants to come over! It would be so nice to cuddle up next to him and just love on him. Okay, I just need to calm down and take it one step at a time. Snap out of it!*

"I was gonna swing by before I go out of town." He spoke casually as if seeing me was no big deal.

Yes, yes, yes! I secretly leaped for joy. *Thank God he can't see me!* I chuckle to myself and try to stay cool.

"Cool, I'll be home, just come on by … whenever." Good, I got it out without stuttering too much or sounding too happy. *Good job girl!* I gave myself a high five.

"Aight, den, I'll holla." He hangs up the phone. Immediately, I jump out of the bed to straighten up my apartment. As small as it is, I keep it pretty clean. It's nothing too fancy, but I wanted to look good and smell good. *My man was coming over in a few hours!*

I mentally prepare a menu in my mind for tonight's dinner. I was thinking that I'd do one of his favorite dishes, stewed chicken with rice and veggies. While the chicken is thawing, I think I will do some laundry and take out the trash. *Oh yeah, and I have to shave my legs and do my eyebrows,* I reminded myself. I can't wait to see him with his fine self. He is tall and brown-skinned with muscles for days. I love his skin; it's so caramel-like. I seem to crave chocolate when I'm around him. His eyes are so dreamy too. I have never seen a black man with hazel eyes before. I make fun of him that his eyelashes are too long for a guy and that he should be in a Cover Girl commercial. He hates it when I tell him that.

I have only known Chris for less than a year. But I feel so close to him and I feel happy and beautiful when I'm with him. No man has ever made me feel that way. I just wish that I could see him more. It seems like he's always preoccupied. But I just know that one day, he will finally commit to me. After all, he did say I was wife material!

I should call Maxine back and tell her I can't make it to choir rehearsal. Mmm … maybe not. I have *so* much to do right now. *Oh well, she will understand.*

Chapter Four

Well, Chris should be here in a few minutes, I thought. *I can't wait to see him.* I didn't bother to call Maxine earlier, so now she's blowing up my phone. I do feel really bad about ditching the choir. *God, I'm sorry, I really am, but I have to be real with you. I really just want to take a break and be with Chris. Is that so bad?*

I want everything to be perfect when he comes over. The chicken is nice and tender, the veggies are nice and buttery, just the way he likes them. I have to make some strawberry grape Kool-Aid; he doesn't like it too sweet. The phone is ringing again; I glance at it. It's Maxine again. Ugh! I know I should answer it, but I just can't right now. Time seems to be moving so fast, and Chris is still not even here. I called him a few times and left him messages and of course I don't get a reply. I suddenly hope that I didn't miss choir practice for no reason. I'm sure he will come tonight; he sounded pretty sure earlier today when we spoke on the phone. I look at the time again. It's almost midnight and he is still not here.

After falling asleep on the couch for almost three hours, I finally came to the conclusion that he's just not coming over. Disappointed, hurt, and feeling very silly and stupid, I turn the stove off and pack up the food and turn off the lights. I'm so angry with myself for believing that he was coming over tonight. *Who does he think he is?* He should have called me at least. I feel horrible. I need to pray for forgiveness. *I should have just gone on to choir practice,* I thought to myself sadly.

As I am praying, I begin to feel worse instead of better. I can't even get my thoughts together. I don't even know what to pray about. *I need forgiveness for everything.* I realized I kept putting this man before God and

my beliefs. My mind seems so jumbled right now, like I can't even think straight or concentrate. *Is this how love feels? Like confusion?* I ask myself. Missing church and choir practice? Putting a man before God? I can't believe what I have become. I change my clothes and get into bed. I was too tired to even bother to cry myself to sleep.

Chapter Five

I awakened to a knock on the door. It's Chris, I know it is. I glance at the clock and I see that it is almost three o'clock in the morning. *What in the world?* I'm about to answer this door and tell him how I feel. But deep down inside, I'm glad that he is here. Even if it is late, or early in the morning, depending on how you look at it.

I decided to swing open the door and try to have on my best "Oh, Negro, I know you not knocking on my door at three o'clock in the morning" look. Chris just moves past me and lets himself in. I try to look angrier, but I don't know if I am doing it right. By the time I close the door, he has his coat off.

"Well, aren't you a little early for dinner?" I spoke sarcastically. At this point, I'm just a tad bit more irritated that he may not know *exactly* what time it is.

Chris comes over to me and gives me a tight hug along with a tender kiss on the lips. I tried not to melt right there. *I need to keep being mad at him so that he knows that he can't just pop up at my house anytime he wants.*

"Oh yeah, I got held up for a few hours," Chris answered casually as he walked over the couch and sits. He has the nerve to beckon me to come over and sit down next to him. I got over there and sit next to him anyway. Hey, what can I say? I wanted those muscular arms around me. But I needed to be strong just a little while longer and let him know that I mean business.

"So do you think it's right for you to just come over anytime you want to or something?" I'm still trying my best to sound angry.

"Man, I told you I got held up," he answered smoothly. I swear he was smirking at me. I loved how Chris playfully tickled me on my side. I quickly snatched his hands away. I was still in my "be-mad" mode.

"So, you're too busy to call me? I know you saw my missed calls, Chris. I hate it when you don't answer my calls." I found myself whining more instead of getting angry. I quickly calmed down and got up from the couch.

"Look, I'm not always by my phone. Plus, you know I don't like talking on the phone. I would rather talk to you in person."

He sounded convincing for some reason. Suddenly, I was melting inside. Maybe we could just cuddle for a while. *There's nothing wrong with that, right?*

"Chris, I waited all night for you. I cooked and everything." I was still trying not to sound whiny, but I couldn't help it.

"Sorry, I just get tied up sometimes. You got some more food left?"

I was about to say: "no", because I was ready to just go cuddle with him. But hey, feed your enemies, right? Reluctantly, I lead him into the kitchen and put a placemat on the table. I fixed him a plate of his favorite dish and a glass of Kool-Aid, no ice, just the way he likes it. Chris ate silently and I just watched him. *Am I in love with him?* I wonder why I am so drawn to him. *He looks so good eating up my food.* My man seemed to be enjoying it!

"Do you want some more?" I asked trying to be polite.

Chris began to lick his fingers and burped. He shook his head. I took his plate from him and poured him another drink. He gulped it down and looked at me and smiled. My heart sank and I smiled back.

"I thought you were supposed to be mad at me, Miss Tami?" he asked, laughing. "The food was great, by the way. You remembered that I like stew chicken with vegetables."

"Of course I did, silly. Did you expect me to forget?" I replied, trying not to blush.

Chris looked at me for a second and then burped again a second and a third time. I would have been turned off by now if it was some other guy, but Chris is so adorable. He wiped his mouth and walked toward me. I was waiting for him to take me into his arms and just kiss me a little. Instead he walked by me, past the living room, and went into the bedroom.

"Where are you going?" I called after him. *How is he just going to walk in the bedroom like it's all good?*

"Going to the bedroom. You coming?" he called back to me.

I sat in the kitchen a little while longer. I let my mind race back and forth. My heart was beating, and there was no denying what I was feeling. I look at the clock on the stove and see that it's almost four o'clock. I'm not going to lie to myself: I can easily predict what is going to happen in the next few minutes. I know that a part of me wants to lie beside him and that a part of me wants him to just leave or at least go on the couch. But I honestly want to go to bed with him and engage into a night of passion. But I can't have sex … not with him. We are not married. I believe that a woman shouldn't have sex until she's married, or at least that's what old people say and that's what the Bible says. And I don't even think that he calls me his girlfriend. *Isn't fornication a sin? The sin of all sins?* I ask myself. *Tami you're capable of just lying next to him.* I won't *do* anything with him. At least I don't think that I will, but I really want to though. *Why lie?*

Chapter Six

The walk from the kitchen to the bedroom seems so long. I felt like I was walking on a tight rope. When I finally got to the bedroom, Chris was already in his light blue boxers and undershirt. He was looking *so* good. I never saw his legs before; they are well defined with muscles and very sexy. My eyes were burning with temptation. I should walk away and go back into the living room. No, better yet, he should just leave and go into the living room if he wants to sleep that bad! I wanted to send him home, and then I wanted him to stay. *But what for?* I have no intention of having sex with him. *I simply refuse to go against my beliefs.* Plus, I don't even know if he feels the same way about me that I do about him. He climbs under the covers and turns off the lamp on the nightstand next to him. I climb into the bed slowly and lay next to him. He wastes no time to wrap his arms around me tightly and pull me close. My breathing seems labored, and I feel like I could be having an asthma attack. I quickly reach over him and turn the lights back on. Chris looks at me and laughs.

"Why you turned the lights back on? You sleep with them on or something?" he asked, seemingly amused. I had to think quickly of what to say to him.

"Yes, I do. I'm scared of the dark." I secretly give myself a high five in my mind. *He should buy that one.*

"Really? You're scared of the dark? That's a new one," he chuckled.

"Oh, so you think I'm lying or something?" I became a little offended. He was still snickering. He leans in and kisses me gently. I return the kiss and allow his hands to wander. I had to admit that I did like the feeling

of his hands exploring me. He broke away after a moment and stared at me genuinely.

"You are so beautiful," Chris said, looking me straight in the eyes. His stare was so intense that I looked away. I wasn't sure how to respond to him so I initiated the next long kiss. This time, to reward him, I allow my hands to explore his body. My heart begins to beat so loud that I can hear and feel the vibration through my ears. I pulled away from him when I felt like I couldn't breathe anymore.

"Baby, what is it?" Chris asked me with that Southern drone of his.

"Nothing," I replied, breaking my hold from him.

"You act like you're scared of me or something."

Maybe I was. My heart was beating too hard. I wonder if he could hear it. I've never been in this position before with *any* guy.

"Look, Chris, you know how I feel about this kind of thing," I was surprised that I was fighting back tears. *Why can't Chris just love me without the sex?*

"What thing?" he sounded confused and aggravated.

"Sex, Chris, sex. You know that this is awkward for me." I tried to explain myself without whining. I still wanted to cry.

"Look, I know you're a virgin or whatever, but come on now. I'm not a stranger. You know me." Chris smiles at me. I'm sure he is hoping that I will change my mind.

"You have to say it like that? I know that I know you, but still. This is hard for me. I mean, I don't know how you feel about me. I hardly see you like I want to."

"Yeah, I know. But Tami, at the same time, you know that it's always been this way." He casually reaches over to me and pulls me close to kiss me again. Just before I decide to kiss him back, a light bulb goes off in my head.

"Chris, are you satisfied with the way things are between us?" I ask curiously.

"Yeah, I mean. We chill and what not ..." Chris replied slowly. He leans down to kiss me again.

"So that's it? We just chill?" I ask impatiently, breaking away from his hold.

"What are you trying to get at, Tami?" he asked with a stone cold attitude.

"I want to know how you feel about me. I hardly see you; you don't call me unless you're coming over. I just want to know if we will ever be more

than this." I sit up on the bed and watch Chris closely. He sighed and stared off into the distance. I could tell he was trying to think of what to say.

"Come over here and lay next to me." He reaches for me and I lay my head on his chest. I wanted to continue the conversation but I felt like I just had to let it go. I didn't want to ruin the moment and upset him. I wanted him to want me the way I wanted him. *I should just have sex with him. If I do, then maybe he will want to see me more and finally see how much I love him*, I thought hopefully. I found myself praying inside my head for some reason. *Lord, please please I don't want to sin against you. But I have a strong feeling that I will. Please please forgive me. I am a sinner saved by grace. I know this is wrong, but it feels so right.*

"What?" Chris's voice startles me. *Oh my gosh! Was I praying out loud?! Oh great! This is so embarrassing.*

"I'm sorry." I had to just give up. There is no way that I can do this. I lean over and I kiss him on the cheek and then on the mouth. I look into his eyes and realize that I had already made up my mind all along about him. For some reason, he looked really different just then. Like he needed someone like me in his life, someone real, someone willing to feel and understand him the way a woman should. I knew right then I was that woman, and I was willing to make that step with him. But I have to know how he truly feels about me first.

"I love you, Chris." I blurted it out in the heat of the moment. I didn't mean to. But it just slipped out. I just knew that Chris would say it back to me. All I heard was the sound of his heavy breathing, and his hands were back under my clothes. When I realized that he didn't say it back, I pulled away from him and looked at him. I'm glad that the lights were still on, because I saw the irritation on his face. I once again interrupted our tender, hot moment. *If looks could kill. I would be dead, he so hates me right now.*

"Did you hear what I just said?" I asked angrily. *Please say it back. Don't make me feel stupid.*

"Yeah, I heard you," he replied steadily, he was still trying to feel me up under my clothes.

"So what is your response to what I said?" I slapped his hands away from me angrily. This was obviously not gonna happen the way I intended it to.

"What? You want me to say it back or something?" he asked, nonchalantly shrugging his shoulders.

"Yeah, I mean, don't you love me?" I asked him. I found myself fighting my tears. I was a little saddened that he was not responding the way I would have wanted him to.

"Look, Tami, I don't want to say anything that may hurt you. I'm not gonna lie to you. I'm just not there yet with you. I don't know if I ever will be," he replied casually.

"Oh, but it's just convenient to let you take my virginity, right?"

Chapter Seven

I got off the bed and passed Chris his clothes. He sits up on the bed and looks at me with the audacity to have a puzzled look on his face.

"What are you doing?" he asks me. The poor thing was so confused. I figured that now is the perfect time for me to be upfront with him.

"Chris, I love you. I really do," I said regretfully.

"I know you do, but I don't want to lie to you." He was still looking *so* fine to me as I watched him getting dressed, but I had to stay focused. *Snap out of it.*

"You know what, Chris? I refuse to keep straddling this fence with you." I stood up straight and tall and spoke my mind. "I can't keep going back and forth with my feelings for you and your lack of feelings for me. I can't keep giving you my all and throw my beliefs out of the window." I had to pause and take a deep breath. "I'm *not* going to have to sex with you, so you need to hurry up and get out." *There I said it, I officially hate myself.*

"So you don't want to have sex with me because I won't tell you what you want to hear? Tami, that's kinda childish, don't you think?" Chris walks over to me and stands in front of me as if I am going to realize how foolish I'm being and change my mind. *For his information, I will not realize how foolish I'm being!*

"You know what? I *almost* gave myself to you, thinking that perhaps you do love me the way that I love you, but now I see that you would have just been taking advantage of me like you always do. I have boundaries you know." The angrier I got, the more tears began to fill up in my eyes. I refused to let him to see me cry.

"Hey, look, I'm not forcing you to do anything. You were just as willing to go there with me, so don't try to make this about me."

"You're right, Chris, I won't make this about you," I retorted. "As a matter of fact, I'm making this about me and taking my life back. I will no longer center my life, my feelings, or my self-esteem around you!" *I showed him!* I stormed into the living room and grabbed his coat for him. *I'm so done with him!* I screamed to myself.

"Well, okay then, take your life back then. I never asked you to change your life because of me. It's not like I was your man." Chris struck a chord with me right then. *How dare he talk to me that way?*

"Okay, since you're not my man, you can leave now, and don't bother coming back either. I was doing fine all by myself before you came along!" I shouted.

"So what are you saying?" He was still sounding confused, and I am not sure what part he is confused about.

"I am basically telling you that I won't have sex with you—*ever!* I'm also saying that I don't want you in my life. It's time for me to be true to myself and what I believe in." I took a deep breath and allowed only one tear to fall. "No man, not even you, is worth me compromising who I am." I was hurt, saddened, angry, and disappointed all at the same time. The realization set in that Chris didn't love me and that I almost had sex with him—a man who didn't love me, a man who didn't deserve me. *He is still so fine though, what a waste of a specimen.* I shook my head in remorse for him.

"Well, I can't knock you for that. I guess it is what it is." Chris said shrugging his shoulders.

I felt really good about myself for the first time in a long time. I cannot believe I was turning Chris—the finest man ever—down. But at the same time, I was proud that I stood up for myself and my beliefs. I felt like Chris needed to move a little faster out of my house and out of my life, for good this time.

"Yeah, it is. This isn't right for me. You're obviously not right for me. I do love you, Chris, but I just realized that you don't value me. I can't lean on you to respect me or love me. I have to do that myself," I explained calmly.

"So basically, you're mad because I won't lie to you and tell you that I love you?"

Chris was seriously asking me this question?

Chris was about to open the door when I decided to make it clear for him. Politely, of course.

"I'm simply choosing to follow God now. I have lost touch with who I am. I'm choosing to cross over the fence and stay there. No more straddling the fence for me. I can't keep living a double life." Chris frowned at me as if it wasn't registering in his brain what I was telling him.

"I have to make better choices for myself," I said proudly. "Getting rid of you will be the first good decision that I'll make. Goodbye, Chris, it was nice knowing you and loving you while it lasted. One day, I will hear a man say those words to me and until then …I would rather wait for God to send Mr. Right."

Chris didn't say anything. He just walked out of the door. He didn't seem mad, just maybe confused more than anything else. I felt bad for him, but not for long. *I did the best thing for myself and my relationship with God. The best thing for me to do was to let him go and to go my way.*

I watched him walk out my life, for good this time. The other side of the fence seemed lonely as I locked the door and walked back to the bedroom. Lying on the bed, the tears I was holding back streamed down my face. *I could have lost my virginity tonight to Chris. I wanted to.* I discovered that he didn't even love me. He didn't even have the nerve to lie to me, at least. I mean, I did want the truth of course, but I didn't want to end up hurt either. I suppose it's better to be hurt now than later on. I was tired, but for some reason, I couldn't fall asleep. I reached over and took my Bible out of the drawer. I opened it up and turned to Psalms 6. Now I can finally pick up where I left off.

Over the Fence: Part 2

I haven't seen Chris for a few months—five months and seventeen days, to be exact. I have to admit that I do look for him sometimes. Not that I'm trying to get back with him or anything. I simply just want to see him, just to see how he would react to me if he saw me. I wanted to see if I had any impression on him since the night I kicked him out of my apartment. I must admit that was a bold move I had made. Sometimes I wondered what it would have been like if I did actually go all the way and have sex with him. I do miss him sometimes, but hey, life goes on, right?

Since giving Chris the boot, I got back in church, I'm reading my Bible everyday, praying every chance I get, and faithfully attending choir practice. I did apologize to Maxine for leaving her hanging, but I didn't bother to give her an excuse as to why I put the choir on the back burner. Of course, she asked me if there was anything going on, and I simply said: "no." It felt good to be back in good with God. I even started fasting and I tithe regularly. I feel so much more complete now, and I want to stay that way too. I vowed to myself that I would never let my integrity be tarnished by a man (or anyone, for that matter). I have to stay true to myself no matter what. But I have to be real: I find myself wondering about Chris sometimes.

Chapter Eight

Waking up for church used to be a hassle, but now I get up knowing that in about a hour, I am going to be in the presence of God and feel his power. I always get excited about that because when I go to church, I release my burdens and I leave them there. The environment at Worship and Deliverance Church of Truth is truly unique in its own way. Whenever I'm there on stage singing, it's like I feel the spirit of God cleansing me and making me a new person, a new woman. Today, I'm singing a duet with Maxine and I'm excited about the song because I love to sing with Maxine; our voices blend together so well. It had been years since we actually did a duet together.

This Sunday, I decided to celebrate myself by wearing my Sunday best. I went into the deepest part of my closet and pulled out my favorite brown-and-tan floral dress with the matching shawl. I was even more excited to match it up with my brand-new cream stilettos. I thought the modest yet youthful-looking dress went well with newly short-cut hair and lightly planted tan-and-gold makeup around my beautiful brown eyes.

Oh yes, I was ready to make my way into church this Sunday and do my thang for the Lord. For so long, I was bound down by the imagination of a man I thought existed. Chris is finally history in my life. Now I know he just wasn't the man for me. I know that because God would not send me just any ol' body to be my husband. He would send me someone who loved me and admired me for sticking to my beliefs.

Arriving at church, I was greeted outside by the choir members, who sincerely commented on my outfit and new haircut. We chatted and laughed our way through the church doors. Maxine met us inside and looked at me with gleaming eyes.

"Girl, you know you wearing that dress, right?" Maxine says as she hugs me. The rest of the choir told me they would head on to the back as they greeted her marching by.

"Thank you so much. You're looking awesome this morning, too," I replied smiling from ear to ear.

"I am so excited about today's duet! Pastor has invited Bishop Tellman and his church too girl—along with some other people I never even heard of. It's about to be packed out today," Maxine explained. I could hear a little bit of nervousness and excitement in her voice.

I had to admit I am a little scared too. *No, no, I am not scared. God did not give me a spirit of fear. I will have no fear,* I prayed to myself silently.

"You not nervous, are you?" Maxine asked, interrupting my thoughts.

"No, girl. Of course not, just ready to get it over with. We been practicing this song for ages, it seems like!" I said with excitement.

Maxine chuckled and suggested we head back to the choir room for our final rehearsal before service.

I looked at my watch; it was almost noon. Praise and worship always lasted extra long. Service never started on time, and I didn't expect it to. I actually enjoyed praise and worship; it was a special time during the week that I allow the music and praise to consume me and actually feel the love of God around me. I began to thank God for taking me through everything I had gone through so far this year, and asking Him to forgive me for my sins. I thanked Him for my job and for my car, my house, my friends, and for my life. God has truly made a way for me always. I let my mind run on Chris for a second. The second turned into minutes. *God, why am I thinking about him?* I asked myself. I blocked the thought from my mind and quickly began to concentrate on the music.

By the time I snapped out of it, I felt a shove of the usher beside me. Mother Johnson was trying to move me out the way as one of the choir members caught the Holy Ghost and cleared my whole row out. Apparently, I was the last one standing. It seemed like I was the only one in the row who hadn't caught the spirit yet. I felt bad; I feel like I missed it. I quickly got back into praise mode and let my mind

desperately seek God for His touch. I let the music rock my soul. I couldn't help but let my mind and body move and scream out to God and praise Him. I know I was cute this Sunday, but I wanted to feel God so bad this morning that I didn't realize my shawl was being stomped all over. The touch I was yearning for finally came in through the pit of my stomach. I began to scream and cry. When it was over with, I was on the floor along with everyone in my row. We had succumbed to the glory of God that morning.

I don't know how long we had been out for, but the pastor prolonged the tithes and offering so that we could all get ourselves together. I gathered my Bible and notebook and prepared my offering, all while trying to straighten my clothes and fix my hair. I knew my makeup was done for. Mother Johnson had laid my shawl across my waist and handed out napkins to the people in my row.

By the time it was our turn to walk to the offering pail, I was as good as new. Walking up to drop off my offering, I noticed the church was very full, more than usual. As I was walking by, I noticed a few people I knew. We quickly exchanged hellos and hugs as we passed by each other. My smile was plastered on my face, and I was enjoying my time in the Lord.

I was almost to the choir stand when I noticed a man who resembled Chris standing at the end of the pew toward the back. He was tall and was fair-skinned just like him. He had on a colorful sweater with dark slacks. His appearance stuck me so hard that I had a nervous knot in my stomach.

I had to gather myself, and I didn't have time. The pastor had prayed over the offering, and now the choir had to walk all the way to the front of the church to get assembled for our song selections. I dared myself not to look back as I had to turn around and walk in the other direction I just came from. *God, please don't let me turn into a pillar of salt,* I prayed silently. I glanced back. I just had to know if that was Chris or a really, really, really fine stranger. Just as I was about to get a clear look at the man, Maxine blocked my view. *Shoot!*

"Girl, I'm right behind you! I figured you were looking for me!" Maxine shouted. *Boy, was she wrong, and man, was I was irritated with her for blocking my view—my only chance to see who that guy was. God, please help me with my attitude right now. I mean now, Lord!*

My spirit was being tested as we were singing the songs during service. I had to force myself to stay focused. Luckily, I was able to pay attention

to the cue for my solo part. I sang as if my life depended on it. I was a little shaky at first, but I made up for it with a high note and little rolling here and there.

> *Lord please, wash me,*
> *Wash me so I'm white as snow.*
> *Only you can do that for me.*
> *Please just wash me, wash me clean.*
> *I was made to please you, Lord.*

I was into the song and what I was saying but my mind was on Chris. *Why? God help me,* I prayed to myself, *Tami, pull it together. You don't have time for this.* Maxine finally came in and sang her part beautifully. I envied her for a few moments and then repented. I have no idea what was going on with me at this moment. This Sunday was supposed to be perfect. *Why wasn't it all of a sudden?*

Chapter Nine

I found myself in a rush to get home after church. I really needed time alone with God. I must admit, I did find myself looking for the guy in the sweater. I also had to admit that I hoped it was Chris. I'm not sure exactly why. Or maybe I just won't admit to myself why I am really hoping it was him. I was disappointed that I didn't see him. Everyone kept stopping me to tell me how great I looked and how anointed my voice was. I politely smiled and kept my eyes peeled for the man I desperately wanted to see once more, just to see if it was in fact Chris. *Chris.* I immediately knew I was playing with the devil.

I had to get Chris out of my mind. I needed to stop thinking about what would have been and what isn't right now. *Lust, back up off me,* I pleaded. *Chris is not worth my salvation. No man on this earth is.* I laid myself on my bed and began to pray. I prayed and cried until I became angry. In the midst of my tears and prayers, I know that God wanted me to admit that I was lonely and tired of feeling like I was losing out on a man's love. *Yes, God, I admit it. I am lonely and tired of coming home alone. I want a companion, someone you chose for me.*

The Sunday that was supposed to be so perfect was turning out to be a nightmare. *God, please help me to get over this. Please help me to just forget about him!* I prayed and cried some more. I just wanted to melt into a little hole until I could get my mind together. *I am useless to the world, my ministry. I just can't get it right. I'm on top one moment and then the next moment, I'm in the gutter again. Why?*

Chapter Ten

I woke up to the sound of my phone ringing. I wasn't going to bother it, as I saw that the call was restricted. I never answer restricted calls, because it's usually a bill collector. My head popped back up. Bill collectors don't call on Sundays. I grabbed the phone and answered it out of curiosity and confusion.

"Hello?" I cleared my throat, trying not to wake too much, because I have every intention of going back to sleep.

"I was just about to put the phone down." It was an unfamiliar male voice on the other end.

"I'm sorry, who is this?" I asked, impatiently.

"It's me, Tami."

Me who? I wanted to ask. I should have asked that. But I already knew who it was: Chris Brennen. *Of all the times he could have called me, why now? Why?*

"Chris?" I was trying not to sound excited, even though I was, I had to admit pitifully. I was trying not to pay attention to how sexy he sounded on the phone.

"Yeah, girl, why you try'na to pretend you don't know who it is?" he replied, chuckling softly. It was weird for me to hear him like that, because I never heard him chuckle before. I don't remember him being that personable. Confusion and irritation set in. I didn't have time for games and I ready to get off the phone.

"Why are you calling me?" I asked, impatiently. I was trying very hard not to sound too harsh, but the curiosity was a flickering light in my head that wouldn't stop. I was just crying over this man a few hours ago. I was

in a bad mood over this guy on my perfect Sunday. I didn't feel like being nice to him for some reason. But then I realized that I must keep a gentle, godly attitude, no matter what.

"I ... I ... well, I just wanted to say hello. I saw you earlier today in church. I didn't get a chance to-"

"You *saw* me?" I interrupted. *So it was you I saw in church today*, I confirmed silently to myself. I wanted to stay in control and not get too excited.

"Yeah, I did. Can I come see you today? We have a lot of catching up to do."

What? Did he just ask to come over? I don't think so. I need to be in control. Who does he think he is? I thought bitterly. *He can't just come over whenever he feels like it.*

"Chris, I don't know about that. I haven't spoken to you or seen you in months. I just don't want to open doors that should be closed." *Good on you, girl!*

"I know. Look, I know I messed up. I know I treated you wrong. I just wanted a chance to make all that better. Is that so bad to do? I mean what about forgiveness and having a gentle attitude towards others?" He certainly sounded different. He sounded a little biblical. *Was he quoting scripture or making fun of me? Hmm, that's funny I was thinking the same thing in my mind. I do need to forgive him and have a gentle attitude towards him.*

"Look, Tami, I just want to see you, that's all. No strings. Just company. Hanging out like we used to do."

The devil. It's the devil, I thought to myself. *I don't want his company. Who does he think he is? No, no, no! I will not fall into this, not again.*

"No, thank you, Chris. I don't want your company, but thank you so much for asking." I said what I had to say as gently as possible.

I pressed *end* on my cell phone as slowly as possible. I guess I was hoping that perhaps I actually would change my mind and come to my senses. I really did want to stay on the phone with him, but I just know that within myself, that I could not let Chris back into my life. I saw the word "restricted" blinking really fast, and then the screen went black and then blank. *I hung up on him. I did it. I'm still in control. I had to do it.* I began to pray to God to transform my mind and for His desires to be my desires. I felt good after I prayed. I changed out of my church clothes, took a shower, threw on my robe, popped in a Tyler Perry movie, and enjoyed a warm bowl of popcorn.

Chapter Eleven

A few hours went by. I had already watched two movies, and now I was going through the opening credits of my third movie. *See? I can enjoy myself without the company of a man.* I chuckled to myself and I threw a handful of chips into my mouth. I found my cozy spot on my couch and wrapped myself up a little tighter in my robe. I loved my robe; it fit like a big old blanket. I was comfortable lying in it with only my undergarments underneath. I was finally into the movie, *What Lies Beneath*, when the phone rang again. I looked at the screen and put the phone down. It was "restricted" again. *If someone wants to really reach me, they can show their number,* I thought to myself. It was probably just Chris anyway. It felt good to ignore his phone calls instead of waiting by the phone for him to call like a dummy. *Never again. I don't think so.*

I pushed *pause* on the movie and ran to the bathroom. I was washing my hands when I could have sworn I heard a light tapping on my door. I turned the water off and listened closely. I still didn't hear anything. *I must be spooked from watching the movie,* I thought. I turned the water back on, and clear as day, I heard knocking at the door. I looked at the clock on the wall and the time read 10:47. *Who had lost their mind to come to my door so late at night?*

I carefully approached the door and looked through the peephole. Standing in the hall was Chris, only it didn't really look like him. Of course, I hadn't seen him in a while either. I didn't realize that I already slowly opened the door and peered at him for a while as he stared back at me. Neither of us said a word for a moment.

"Hey," he finally said.

There was no need for pleasantries or a conversation out in the hall for my nosy neighbors. I let him in and left him at the doorway while I went and sat on the couch.

"Aren't you going to invite me in?" Chris asked, smiling.

I studied his face and realized he *had* changed. He'd lost weight, not a lot, but a noticeable amount. He was also in khaki pants and a collared shirt. His hair was cut and his face was cleanly shaven. I remember him always wearing baggy jeans and a white T-shirt with stubble on his cheeks. Chris was always so fine to me, but looking at him now, he appeared to be very handsome and pleasant-looking. *Dear God, please order my words and my steps,* I prayed silently.

"You *are* inside, Chris. Don't you know what time it is?" I asked coolly.

"No, actually, I don't," Chris replied, stepping inside a little more. "I just got off work and I decided to stop by. I didn't realize what time it may be. I'm sorry to be holding you up from your movie night," he explained in an apologetic tone.

Where is he working this late at night dressed in business casual wear? I wondered, curiously.

"No, it's okay. I was just enjoying a night in. You can come in and sit down over there." I was still choosing my words carefully and staying in control. I even made sure he specifically sat across from me and not next to me. "So, where are you working at now?" I asked. I really didn't care; I just wanted to control the conversation. I wanted to be in control of everything.

"I have my own cleaning business and lawn-care service. I had to check on some of my employees at one of the office buildings. The van broke down again." Chris chuckled again and met my gaze as if he wanted to study my expression. I kept my face as straight as I could. I was definitely impressed though. *His own business? Two businesses, to be exact.*

"What have you been up to these days?" he asked, smiling at me.

I wondered if he was really happy to see me or putting up a front. I made sure I didn't crack a smile, because I didn't want him to see me melting on the inside. I was in awe of how incredibly handsome he was looking and how accomplished he had become in less than six months.

"Well, you know, the same old, singing in church, working at the hospital as a Patient Intake Clerk, the usual," I responded, keeping it short and simple. *Stay in control, Tami, hold it together and no, do not smile,* I told myself.

"Tami, I heard you sing today at Worship and Deliverance you sounded really good! I never knew you could sing like that!" Chris said with the biggest I had ever seen on his face.

"Thanks. I've been singing all my life. I didn't even see you there," I lied. I didn't want him to know that I may have *thought* I saw in him in church today. I still wanted to stay in control and not let him notice that I was blushing.

"Yeah, I was there. You sounded great today; you gave me chills." He grabbed his arms and pretended that he was cold.

"Yeah, that was me." I sounded so stupid. *God, what is going on? What have you done with him?* I smiled back at Chris. I was so flattered that he loved my voice so much that it gave him chills! I'm also thrilled that I actually saw him at a church service!

"Who did you go to church with today?" I asked. The atmosphere was loosening up a little bit, and I was enjoying his company. It was like seeing an old friend that had come into town, instead of an estranged lover.

"I went with my uncle. He was invited by your pastor; they play golf together or something. I didn't get to stay for the whole thing. I had to head back to the office to handle some matters. But I enjoyed it, though. The praise and worship was great. I really liked it." My ears were burning with pleasure. This was too good to be true. I truly felt like God was linking us back together. Only this time, Chris was a gentleman and he seemed so genuine.

"That's really good. I'm glad that you enjoyed the service. Hopefully, you will come visit us again sometime," I said hopefully.

"I just may visit again. I felt at home. It's been awhile since I been in a good church home," Chris replied, nodding his head. "Maybe I can go with you sometime?" he suggested. Chris and I caught each other's gaze until I broke the silence by offering him something to drink. *Take your time, talk slow, Tami.*

"Sure, that would be great. I love my church. I have been there for a few years now," I said as I poured him a drink.

As I was in the kitchen, I realized I was in my bathrobe the whole time. Blushing and suddenly uncomfortable, I quickly gave Chris his drink and swiftly walked back into my room to put on my really thick two-piece pajama set. I certainly didn't want Chris to have any ideas while he was here in my house.

I walked back to the living room. Chris was really into watching the movie. He saw me coming in and looked up at me.

"I can't believe this guy. I think he killed that girl. I put money on it." He laughed and went back to the movie.

I wanted to ask him what he was doing here, but his company was so refreshing that I wasn't sure if I even wanted to know, or if it even mattered. *Chris has actually changed in a good way,* I observed.

"Would you like some more juice?" I asked as I went into the kitchen to pour my own drink.

"No, thank you. I'm good, actually," Chris responded with his eyes glued to the movie.

I sat down on the couch with my drink and we watched the movie, occasionally making small conversation. Although I was watching the movie, I wasn't really paying attention to it. I sneaked a peek at my watch; it was well past midnight. Definitely ungodly hours. The movie was almost at an end, and I was unsure of what was supposed to happen next. I was enjoying his visit, but I didn't want him to think that he was welcome to be in my house all night either.

"I can't believe how crazy this movie is. Harrison Ford is the man!" Chris shouted excitedly.

"I didn't know you like Harrison Ford movies," I said, laughing. I didn't take Chris as a scary-movie kind of guy or a Harrison Ford fan at that.

"Really, I just love movies. I hardly have time to sit at home and watch a movie anymore with everything going on at work and all."

"Yeah, I know what you mean. I finally got a couple days off from work to just enjoy being at home." I found myself yawning, and my stomach started growling.

"Oh my goodness, how could I be hungry this time of night?" I asked myself out loud. Without thinking, I foolishly asked Chris if he would like a sandwich. *Darn it, Tami! You and your big mouth!*

"Um, yeah, sure, if it wouldn't be any trouble. I am a little hungry." He looked at me gratefully, and I couldn't believe my eyes when he got up and picked up the cups and walked them in the kitchen along with my popcorn bowl. He even picked up the popcorn pieces that I had left on the floor and on the table. I was so astonished that I didn't mean to stare at him. *What was the catch?* I immediately put my guard up; I made myself believe that the old Chris was in there, and I just wish he would just come on out and stop wasting time. This gentlemanly stuff was just too good to be true.

"Do you want ham or turkey or both?" I yelled from the kitchen.

"However you make it is fine with me. I'm not picky about my sandwiches." Chris replied.

"Okay, cool, I'll just do a basic toast sandwich then. You can go ahead and put in a new movie if you want. I have Ace Ventura on the table already; you can never go wrong with Jim Carrey." Chris and I laughed, and he put the movie in while the sandwiches were toasting slowly. We both were yawning and laughing at the same time during the first scene of the movie. It was certainly way past my bed time.

"I think the bread is finally ready. I'll be right back with the food," I said. I jumped up and ran into the kitchen. My stomach was growling so loudly that I had to get something to drink.

I fixed the sandwiches and refilled our glasses with juice. I decided to take Chris's food out first. I walked by him and put the food on the table.

"Well, here you go; the sandwich is finally done. My toaster is kinda slow," I explained. When I didn't hear a response, I realized he had fallen asleep. I didn't expect that at all. I also had no idea what to do with him. *Do I wake him?* I wondered to myself. His breathing was very soft and peaceful. His now-slender features made him look even more handsome than I remembered.

Every apparent good quality I could hope for him to have, he displayed tonight. I didn't even bring up the fact that I was ignoring his phone calls tonight. I was actually glad that he just popped up. *Maybe he missed me and wanted to make up for the way he had treated me before. I probably shouldn't wake him up. He must have had a long day, to fall asleep to a Jim Carrey movie.* I put his food back in the kitchen. I dimmed the lights in case he woke up so that he could see his way out. I wasn't expecting him to still be here in the morning.

The thought of waking up to him and inviting him to lay in the bed with me crept in. *He has been a gentleman so far, right? No, no, no, don't even go there. I pleaded with myself. God, I just want to do what's right, and the right thing to do would be to send him on home right now. But it's so late, almost two in the morning.* I covered him with a blanket and decided to take his shoes off to make him more comfortable. *This is going above and beyond the call of duty here,* I thought to myself. I know the gesture was a little more than friendly, but I just wanted to do something nice for him. *Why? Because I like the guy.*

I suddenly had no appetite to eat my sandwich. I didn't have the strength to wrap them up and put them in the fridge. I walked back to

my room alone. I know I was doing the right thing. I had to leave Chris where he was. If I asked him to come back in the room with me, I would be compromising all the beliefs I worked so hard to keep all my life—well, actually the past five months and seventeen days. Chris just wasn't that special, to break all my commandments. Thank God that I was too tired to even stay up and listen for him to see if he had left yet. I did fall asleep during my meditation. This was the first night in a few months that I hadn't read a Bible verse before I went to sleep. I vowed to at least read it before lunchtime tomorrow, to make up for not reading it tonight.

Chapter Twelve

I woke up the next morning and stretched both my arms out and lay there for a moment. I let my mind think about everything that had happened last night and wondered if it was a dream after all. I popped my eyes opened and ran into the living room. Chris was gone. My heart sank a little bit. I don't know why, but I expected him to be here. It was well after ten o'clock. He probably had to go to work or something. I did notice a piece of paper hanging on the table. Looks like Chris left me a note. I opened the folded paper and his handwriting was surprisingly neat.

> *I didn't want to wake you this morning, you looked so peaceful. I did eat my sandwich and had a cup of juice. It was really good to see you last night. Although I know at first you didn't want to see me ☺. I want to treat you to lunch. I know you said you don't go to work today, so I will pick you up around noon. I know you don't have any plans for the day (lol). Later.*

I read the note at least three times. This was all just happening too fast. Chris said he actually wanted to take me out for lunch? He actually knows me well enough to know that I didn't have any plans! I have less than two hours to get ready! I tore my bedroom apart looking for the right thing to wear. I need to be "dressy" casual to be prepared for anything. *Where will he take me? Mickey D's? The King? Maybe he will take me somewhere upscale,* I thought excitedly to myself. My mind was racing with the possibilities of where we would go on our first date. *Date? No, this is not a date,* I reminded

myself. *We are just friends. No big deal.* It was almost 11:15, and Chris was supposed to be here in forty-five minutes. I had put on some black pants and a sage green shirt that I dressed up with my jewelry and low heels. My hair was well polished brushed down salon style. *I feel like a movie star getting ready for the Academy Awards!*

I was pacing back and forth, waiting for the phone to ring, waiting for him to call me. I stopped in my tracks, realizing that I hadn't read my Bible or prayed all day. *This is not like me,* I thought somberly. *I'm letting myself get distracted already. Not good.* I hadn't even read my Bible last night. I'm letting Chris get in the way again. I can't do that. I have to find a happy medium. No, no compromise. *I cannot and will not serve God and man!* No way. Not Chris anyway. *I can't fall for him again,* I said to myself sadly.

I need to be strong. I immediately went into the living room with my Bible. I turned to Romans and began to read. I skipped and skipped the pages trying to find something to connect to, something to stand out and speak to me. I found nothing. Nothing. *God, please I need your word right now. I need your word, please.* I finally came across Psalms 46, verse 10: "Be still and know that I am God."

"Okay God, I understand," I said out loud. "I will wait on you and be still. I take my hands off this situation. I don't want to do anything outside of your will." I sat down on the couch and gazed at the ceiling.

My stomach started to growl at noon on the dot. I managed to save my appetite for my lunch "outing" with Chris. I decided that it would be best to proceed with the outing with as little expectation as possible. I watched as the clock read ten minutes past the hour. Of course, he may be a little late. Maybe he was at work. My phone remained silent. I made sure the ringer was turned up so that I could hear it ring. I tried not to pace too much. I went over to the window to see if I needed a coat or a sweater. Although it was September, the weather seemed to still be unpredictable. *Yup, I should definitely bring a coat.* I thought to myself. I opened the window and noticed a gray Acura speed up to the curb. A man got out of the car quickly and ran inside. I almost broke my neck to see who it was.

A few minutes later, I heard a knock at the door, and I knew it was Chris. I grabbed my coat and tried not to swing the door open too quickly.

"Well, hello there," I greeted him coolly. I managed to hold my excitement and irritation at him being late simultaneously.

"Sorry I'm late. I left my phone at the office, or else I would have called to tell you I was running late," he explained half way out of breath.

I looked him up and down quickly. He wore black slacks with a striped sweater and white collared shirt. *Nice. Really nice,* I thought to myself because I refuse to give him compliment out loud.

"No problem. Ready to go?" I asked.

"Yup."

We took the elevator and walked outside. Chris's gray Acura was clearly brand new. The new leather smell on the inside out did my vanilla perfume for sure. It was also very clean on the inside. *His car definitely makes my two-door Toyota look like small change.* I caught my ungratefulness and rebuked it under my breath. *I'm absolutely thankful for everything that God has provided for me thus far.*

"What did you say?" Chris asked as he was pulling off.

"Oh, nothing. I was just—"

"Talking to yourself," he said, chuckling.

Chris took us around a few blocks, and we finally stopped at an Italian café. I could feel the excitement build up inside me. He walked over and opened the car door for me. I was trying not to catch his gaze, because I could feel his eyes on me. *I will not fall for him; he is just being nice. It's no big deal,* I urged myself.

Chapter Thirteen

When we got inside the café, the young, dark-haired hostess greeted us with a smile. "Would you guys like a booth or the couples' seating in the private corner?" The hostess called us a couple. I watched Chris out of the corner of my eye. I wasn't sure if I should say that I did want the couples' private booth.

Chris shrugged his shoulders. "The couples' corner would be fine. I don't like to be so close to the door."

The hostess led the way, and I was excited that our seating was intimate and small. Chris waited for me to sit down and get settled in before he sat down. I caught myself smiling. *He just keeps on surprising me,* I thought, happily. The way things were going, I wouldn't mind us being a couple, *but* at the same time, I did need to be on my guard. *I have to remember to keep my cool,* I reminded myself. *Just enjoy your day off and this free lunch along with this fine company*—no pun intended.

I could tell Chris was trying not to look at me directly from across the table. During our conversation, he would keep his head down and look up only briefly. I managed to catch his eyes once or twice. They were still gorgeous. He was still gorgeous. I wonder what he thinks of me.

"You know, Tami, I'm glad that you decided to let me in last night. I know you didn't have the best thoughts of me because of—"

"The past is the past. Let us just enjoy the moment, okay?" I stopped him from apologizing, because there was no point in remembering all the bad stuff when things were going great so far. *Guys always know how ruin a good moment,* I thought to myself.

"Well, okay. I know that you're wondering why I'm a little different than I was before."

Yup, he hit it right on the button. I decided to go there with him. *Hey, why not? He brought it up.*

"Yeah, I did notice a little something different about you. You don't seem like the man I kicked out of my apartment five months ago," I explained with a smile.

"Well, I'm not the same. I don't know. I guess I just grew up a lot the last few months. I realized that I lost a good woman and friend. I wasn't living my life the way a man should. So I decided to grow up. I had been spending a lot of time with my uncle, too. He kinda put me on point to a few things."

I was glad to hear that his uncle was a good influence to him. I was definitely happy about how mature Chris became since we separated. I was proud of him. We ordered our food and drinks and talked some more. Chris didn't mention anything about a girlfriend, so I had to assume he didn't have one, only because he *did* spend the night at my house. But I had to ask just to be sure. "So what about a girlfriend, fiancée, baby mama? Anyone in the picture?" I asked, trying to laugh it off as if it wasn't a big deal if I knew or not.

"Well, no, I don't have a girlfriend. I did think I had a son at one point. I found out after awhile that he wasn't mine."

"Huh?" I was shocked. "You *thought* you had a son?" I asked slowly, making sure I asked the question the way I wanted to, instead of how I felt. My mind began to race, and my heart began to beat a little faster with jealousy, sadness, and disappointment. *He has been with another woman. He has had sex with another woman.* I had to shake my head to snap out of it. *It's not like he loved me anyway. It doesn't even matter, he is here now, and that's what matters.* I finally calmed myself down and tuned back into what Chris was saying.

"A girl I used to date came out of nowhere and told me her son was mine. I actually believed her. The timeline in which she got pregnant was the time that we were together. So I just assumed that, of course, the boy was mine."

I swear I saw the whites of his eyes get a little pink. I believe he was holding back tears. I reached my hand to touch his but I was interrupted as the waitress came by and dropped off my chicken pasta and Chris' shrimp basket. He looked relieved to have a distraction for a moment. I didn't get

to touch his hand. I sighed and began to play with my food. As hungry as I was, didn't have an appetite.

"I spent months with Jaleel after he was born," Chris continued, to my surprise. I made sure I gave him my undivided attention. I was glad that he felt that he could be open with me. I began to put the pieces together and understood why Chris was so distant and unavailable the months before I broke off our relationship. I decided that I wanted him to be with me and only me. I was slowly falling for him again.

"So, I guess you got attached to him, huh?" I asked after I swallowed a spoonful. I wanted him to know that I was interested in what he had gone through.

"Yeah, in a short period of time, we actually got attached to each other," he replied, softly.

"So I guess you were dealing with all of this while we were seeing each other?" I asked carefully.

Chris nodded his head and continued to eat.

"How old is Jaleel now?" I was definitely very curious.

"He's two now. My uncle advised me to get a DNA test, just to be sure of things because Jaleels' mom wanted to take out child support on me. Lucky thing I did, 'cause the test was negative. Jaleel wasn't mine. It broke my heart so bad that I lost weight over it. I couldn't do anything for about a month."

I could tell that Chris was fighting back his tears while he was talking to me. I admired him for wanting to be a strong man, even though he was obviously really hurt. I kept my eyes on him to let him know that it was okay to vent with me. I have no intention of judging him.

"I was torn up about the whole situation. That's why it was hard for me to commit my time to you. I was dealing with a lot during the time. I didn't want to take my hurt on you. So I tried to stay away." Chris looked away from me and continued to eat. We both ate and sipped our drinks in silence for a while. Finally, our eyes met and we both exchanged intense stares that lasted for what seemed like an eternity.

Chris dropped me off at home and promised to call me later. I was certainly looking forward to it. Lunch was awesome. Chris was awesome. The conversation was awesome. I couldn't have asked for anything more. He paid for lunch and even bought me a single rose on the way out of the café doors. *What more could a girl ask for?*

Part 3

Chapter Fourteen

The next few months were heavenly. I was truly smitten by this man who had once hurt me. I didn't care about that anymore because I was much more curious and excited about where we were headed. Every night before we went to bed, I thanked God for sending me a renewed Chris. I even prayed that it was in His will for us to be together as man and wife one day. I have to be honest; it was hard to resist Chris. I loved him with all my heart and soul—so much that I let him take my virginity. I did tell him for about a month or so that I was saving myself for marriage and that was final. Of course, there were days he would try to convince to me to change my mind. Then one day, he said that he loved me more than anything in the whole wide world. I remembered thinking to myself: *Finally! He loves me!*

Some days, I think I should have waited, but why bother delaying us having sex when we are going to be making love with each other for the rest of our lives? I'm the type of woman who knows how to get and keep her man happy by all means necessary. He is, after all, my boyfriend now. Chris is my man, and I want him to always feel like one. I cuddle with him and rub his head until he falls asleep. I cook for him and make sure his clothes are ironed for work. I'm showing him how I could be a good wife. I just hope for the best for us and maybe one day, I will wake up with a ring on my finger, just like the woman in that Tyler Perry movie.

I do get a little frustrated with myself, because no matter how focused I try to stay, I keep missing the mark. I haven't touched my Bible in weeks, although I try to make up for it by at least praying before I go to sleep. Well, at least after Chris falls asleep. I'm too shy to pray around him and I

won't do it out loud like I'm used to. I missed the last two Sundays because I kept waking up late to get ready for church. I set my alarm on Saturday night, but my clock has been "mysteriously" getting unplugged in the middle of the night. Oh well, with work and playing "wifey" all day and night, I could use the extra few hours of rest.

Chapter Fifteen

I came home from work on Monday evening to find almost all the lights in the house on, and Chris cannot be found anywhere in the house.

"How many times do I have to tell this man to turn the lights off in the house?" I shouted out loud, angrily. "The light bill is sky high already!" I screamed. I went around and flicked off all the lights, except for the little light in the living room. *Why in the world were all the lights on?* I was so irritated that I could just scream. I kicked off my shoes and sat on my couch, wondering what my next move should be. I decided to take a shower to get my mind cleared and then figure out what I wanted to eat for dinner. Walking through the house, I saw little bits of Chris's stuff in the house: a sock here and there, undershirts on doorknobs, and different pairs of shoes along the hallway.

Baskets of clothes were also piled up in the corner, and mail was stocked up on the dressers in the bedroom. In the bathroom, there were pants and shoes behind the door and little pieces of hair in the sink, most likely from when he shaved this morning. I was so frustrated with how Chris was treating our home, *my* home to be technical. *My apartment has never been this messy. I'm just not used to sharing my space this way,* I think to myself. I decided that I will need to talk with him later on. I was feeling lonely all of a sudden, and I needed a friend to talk to. I hadn't spoken to Maxine in a while so I dialed her number.

Maxine answered on the second ring. "Hello?" I was really glad to hear her voice.

"Hey, it's me. How are you?"

"Hey, Tami! I'm good. I been calling you since forever, but I never hear back from you."

Maxine's voice appeared to be full of questions and concerns. Yet I knew that she was happy that I called. I feel bad that I never told her about Chris and how we have actually been living together for at least four months. I have never been the type to talk about my relationships, because I am more of a private person.

"Oh yeah, everything is fine. I just been working hard, that's all." I tried to laugh it off, to ease the conversation a little bit.

"Are you sure, girl? Everyone from choir has been asking about you, including the pastor."

I didn't realize I've been gone from the congregation that long for the pastor to notice my absence, I felt ashamed.

"Oh really? I just can't seem to get to my phone these days. I just got home and took a shower, I said to myself: 'I should give Maxine a call, I haven't spoken to her in a while.'" I tried to chuckle a little bit.

"Well, I'm here for you if you need me. You shouldn't be a stranger, girl. You *need* to get back here and start singing again. You know you are too gifted to do nothing with that voice of yours," Maxine said sincerely.

"I know I'm supposed to be singing, Max. It's just that, I haven't ... well, I don't know." I really had no idea what to say. *Why wasn't I singing?* I asked myself. I tried to think back to the last time I actually sang in the shower.

"Girl, you know God gave you that gift for a reason. I have never heard anyone hit a high note like you. You should be making records or something!" Maxine has always been trying to get me to go into a recording studio and do a CD. I don't see myself as a recording artist or a superstar or anything like that. I'm just plain ol' me: a woman who can carry a tune. *What's so great about that?*

"Max, my voice is not all that. I mean, yeah, I can sing, but not like that," I replied.

"Whatever! You can blow, and you need to get back in this choir and help these girls out!" Maxine laughed.

My eyes welled up with tears. I missed having a friend around, someone I could pray with and talk to about my life. I felt like I left my old life behind for a new one with a man who was starting to trash my home little by little. I began to wonder, *There should be more to my life than where I am. But I just don't know what it is.*

"Hey, baby, you on the phone?" I didn't hear Chris come in. I quickly put the phone on mute and hoped that Maxine didn't hear him in the background.

"Yeah I am, just hold on a sec." I took the phone off mute and tried to sound natural.

I apologized quickly. "Sorry about that, Maxine." *Please don't ask me anything,* I begged in my mind.

"Baby, you seen my soap anywhere?" Chris asked from the bathroom. *Ugh! Shut up already!* I wanted to scream.

"Hey girl, I gotta go, but I will try to stop by practice tomorrow, okay?" I was trying not to sound like I was rushing her off the phone. The heat in my body was rising as I heard the shower water running with the door open. All the wrong signals were already noticeable.

"Oh, okay … well, hopefully you will have a chance. I understand if you're busy though." Maxine's voice sounded heavy, as if she wanted to say more but she didn't want to offend me or get in my business.

"Yeah, I will sure try. I hope you have a great night, Max," I said hurriedly.

"Think about what we talked about, okay?" Maxine said.

"I promise I will," I replied sincerely.

We said our goodbyes and hung up.

Chris just blew it for me. Darn! I slammed my head on the pillow and screamed. *God, I don't like how I am feeling right now. I don't understand what's wrong.*

"Hey, you got some lotion?" Chris shouted from the doorway of the bathroom.

I looked up from my pillow and noticed he was standing in the doorway. He was wet—and had no towel on.

"Umm, you need to go put some clothes on, Chris!" I shouted at him and threw him a robe.

"What? You act like this is new to you or something," he chuckled, "Relax, I can't find my towel."

"Oh, please. Just for that, you can sleep on the couch." I threw him two pillows off the bed and turned off the bedroom lights.

"Tami, what's wrong with you? Why you got an attitude with me tonight?" Chris asked me after wrapping himself in the robe.

"I don't feel like talking about it, not right now. I'm just having a moment," I was so aggravated that I could cuss.

"You sure you don't want to talk?" he asked, walking over to the bed. I did feel a little comfort with his hand on my shoulder as he caressed it gently. *God, that feels good,* I thought to myself.

"Chris, do you think I can sing?" I asked him softly. He looked at me bewildered.

"Yeah, you know I do. Why do you ask?"

"I don't know; I was wondering." I shrugged my shoulders and put my hand under my chin.

"You ever wonder what your purpose is in life?" I asked.

"No, not really. I just live my life on purpose, that's all you can do, baby," He shrugged his shoulders and jumped off the bed.

"I just was thinking lately about what my purpose is in life. I wonder if I am actually supposed to be singing in concerts and making records or something." I looked at him as if I was looking for an answer. I waited for something, but I wasn't sure if it was approval or encouragement. *God, I used to look to you for encouragement, now I'm looking at Chris for answers. How in the world can he help me?* I thought to myself.

"Baby, you seen the lotion?" Chris asked as he was digging around on the dresser. While he was searching for the lotion, he was knocking over my spray bottles and ornaments on the dresser.

"Chris, you're knocking over my things!" I shouted as I jumped off the bed, "Maybe you would find things if you didn't have them everywhere!" I continued to shout. Chris walked away and I would have followed him to the bathroom, but I had no energy or intention of having another argument with him. Sometimes I have to remind myself to snap back into reality. I am trapped in a situation that I suddenly was afraid to get out of. I didn't want to lose Chris by complaining about everything all the time. I could just clean up tomorrow since I didn't have to work. *No big deal, right?*

Chapter Sixteen

Chris woke up this morning and left for work a little later than usual. I was relieved to see him go. I needed some time to myself to get my house back in order. I put on a worship CD for the first time in weeks and cleaned my house while singing along with my favorite gospel artists. I was impressed with how good I was sounding. My voice started out to be a little raspy at first, but the more I sang, the better I sounded. I picked up the broomstick and pretended it was a microphone. I closed my eyes and imagined that I was on stage in front of millions of people. I imagined myself worshipping God as I sang. I saw people singing along to my music crying and worshipping God. The song was over with, and my eyes were still closed as I sang a verse of the song a capella. I was impressed with myself. I sounded better than ever! *Maybe my purpose is to sing after all,* I thought.

I allowed God to minister to me through the peace I was feeling in the atmosphere. I began to pray and ask God for forgiveness for not talking to Him as much as I know I should. I even asked Him to reveal to me what I needed to do to get closer to Him. Tears began to well up in my eyes. I cried, sang, worshipped, and cleaned up for more than an hour.

It was almost two o'clock in the afternoon when I got done cleaning. I still had a few hours until Chris came back from work. I decided it would be a good time to head over to the church and visit Maxine.

Chapter Seventeen

I knew I would find Maxine in the choir room working on new material. Choir was her life and I think I envied her a little bit for walking in her calling more than I ever was. She seemed to just have it all together. Maxine is definitely a woman of purpose who knows what she wants and goes after it with all her heart and soul. I know for myself now that I have been called to minister to people through my singing, but I haven't been walking in my calling at all. I sat down in the back of the choir room, waiting for Maxine to notice me. It could be awhile, because she was into playing the piano, going up and down the keys, trying to match the keys to the song. Her voice was so beautiful and pure. I found it a treat to be able to sit down and hear her singing.

It was no effort for Maxine to just sing a song and God's presence would be in the room. I could honestly say that Maxine was a worshipper, not a singer. In other words, Maxine sings to glorify God and not to show off or try to sound good. *What was I? Do I worship or do I sing?* I asked myself. Tears were beginning to well up my eyes, and I knew a depression was coming on. *God, I don't know what's going on with me. I don't know what to do. I mean, I do know what to do, but I don't think I have the energy or the will to do it. Why is this so hard for me?* I asked God. *Why me? Things used to be so easy for me.*

"Hey there!" Maxine called from across the room. She left the piano and walked swiftly over to me. Even though Maxine was in her late thirties, she could certainly pass for someone in her mid-twenties. She was a little taller than me. Although her waistline was thick, she wore her weight well. I always loved how she kept her bob cut so neatly. I don't think

I have ever Maxine without her hair done nicely. She was always dressed to impress, with flawless makeup on her fair skin. I quickly wiped my eyes before Maxine made her way to the back row where I was. I even tried to crack a smile, but I knew I already gave myself away. I looked down at my shirt and I saw that my collar was soaked with my tears.

"I sure am surprised to see you!" She greeted me happily. "I just came in between lunch breaks to work on some music. What brings you by today?" Maxine's smile slowly faded away because she was already reading that something was wrong with me. I looked at her, and I knew that I needed someone to talk to. It seemed like my prayers were hitting a ceiling. *How can I even talk to God in my state of mind?* I asked myself, sadly. "You can talk to me, Tami. You know I don't judge," Maxine said softly as she reached out to hold my hand.

I took a deep breath and spilled my guts about Chris, from beginning to end. While I was talking to her, I looked at her face to see if there was any sign of her thinking that I sounded stupid, but her face always remained with compassion and understanding. I was relieved to finally get it all out. *I never told anyone about Chris before. He was my hidden secret. Now I was exposed.*

"Wow, I had no idea you were dealing with all of this." Maxine took a deep breath and shook her head. "It's amazing how one minute we are on one road with God, and the next minute, we make a wrong turn and we seem to be on the road all by ourselves," Maxine smiled and she shook her head again as looked at me. She gripped my hand even tighter. "I was in your shoes once with a guy I thought I was so in love with. I just knew God sent him just for me. No one could tell me any different." She took a deep breath and continued. "We were in love, or at least I thought that's what love was." Maxine held her head down for a moment and then looked at me intensely.

"I know you see me and you think that I have it all together," she said, "Everyone seems to assume that because I don't talk about my troubles that I don't have any or that I'm not dealing with anything at all," Maxine explained. "The pastor, the church family, and everyone else rely on me for many things because they know they can depend on me. I work a full time job, go to school part time, and take care of my sister's children while she works at night. But people don't know that I have to keep myself prayed up just to hold on, just to make it another day." She paused and let go of my hand. There was a bit of sadness in her face.

For as long as I have known Maxine, she was always smiling, laughing, or giving someone a word of encouragement. I couldn't imagine her going through anything in her own life because she never acted as if things were wrong in her life. I felt foolish and immature. *How could I think that about anyone? We all have struggles.*

"I know this may sound strange, but I want to be like you, Maxine. You're an example of who a true woman of God," I said truthfully.

"See, that's the thing," she said harshly. "That's what you *see*, but what if I told you that I'm a recovering heroin addict and that I have been living with HIV for the past six years?" Maxine found my eyes and looked at me for an answer. I was lost for words for the moment. *HIV? Heroin? Maxine?* Nothing was adding up for me. *What do I say to that?*

"I- I … I don't know what to say. I had no idea." I sat silently for a moment. Maxine looked off into the distance with hardly any emotion.

"The man I was so in love with introduced me to heroin. We never did needles until one day he wanted me to prove my love to him by sharing one. Of course, I knew the risks of using needles. I saw the warnings in commercials, bulletin boards at school, pamphlets, I heard stories about people living with AIDS, but I did it anyway. I didn't care; my love for him was stronger than what any drug or disease could do to me." Maxine looked at me straight in my eyes.

I understood exactly the kind of love Maxine was talking about. I loved Chris in that crazy way too. I allowed myself to compromise my beliefs for him. I felt filthy. *How could I let myself fall so short?* I felt horrible. Being a virgin and not giving myself to a man who was not my husband used to be my trademark.

"I do love Chris, Maxine, I really do. But I still feel empty. I feel like if I let him go, I will regret it like I did the first time. I was angry that I let him go. I felt like I was losing something or missing out on something, but I had no idea what I was losing. I felt like I was in control and I didn't want him to take that away from me."

"What happened after you let him go?" Maxine asked.

I thought about it for a moment. "Well, I was going to work, church, the usual … nothing special," I replied.

"Exactly, You were going to church and what else? I bet you were praying more, reading your Word more, singing better than ever, eating right, and although you were lonely, you were content in God, right?"

Maxine really made a good point. Although I was angry with myself for letting Chris go, God had become my source of light and peace. *It was*

so true! When I wasn't with Chris, I was with God. Naturally, there was a disconnect with God during my relationship with Chris, one that was noticeable to me in every way. I realized that as long as I was with Chris, I would be stifling my relationship with God and turning away from Him on purpose.

"Yeah, that's true, Maxine. Since I have gotten back with Chris, I haven't been able to grow spiritually the way I desire to. It's when I am not around him that I am able to do everything I used to love to do, like sing and write songs. It's so strange how that happened to me. I try to even it out and do both, but I can never find a happy medium between my natural relationship and my spiritual relationship." *Because you're not supposed to,* I reminded myself. *You cannot serve God and man at the same time.*

The pain in my heart was deeper than I had imagined it would be. I let Chris take a hold of my world once more. The control that I had was nonexistent as long as he was around. *So what shall I do about it?* I looked at Maxine, and I didn't see a woman living with HIV or a woman who used to be hooked on heroin. All I saw was a woman walking with God, and I realized that His favor was all over her. I realized she didn't look like a sick woman. Ironically, she looked like a healed woman.

"Tami, let me tell you something. You have a voice that could melt chocolate in a freezer. Your gift is nothing but God-given. So is mine. That is why our gift comes with a price. We were anointed by God to put our pain and suffering into our music to *deliver* other people. But with that price comes decision-making. We have to be more careful than others of the decisions we make, because the devil is busy and he is out to destroy the vulnerable. Don't be one that he can destroy. Think about that." Maxine grabbed my hand again and held on to it tightly.

My anointing comes with a price. Yes, it does. The price of uncertainty, the price of failure, but I can change that if I want to. Only if I want to.

"I know this a lot for you, especially when you're in a dark place that you can't see yourself out of. But you know the word that's over your life. My testimony goes beyond just being a junkie and ending up with HIV. Would you believe that Marcus died with AIDS, herpes, and a heart condition?" Maxine asked me with intense eyes. I was frozen in place. She shook her head and started laughing.

"You don't understand, Tami. I should have died from those diseases too, but God spared me with only HIV. The tests say that I have HIV, but the doctors can't find anything wrong with me. I have the disease but no symptoms of the disease or traces of it. Do you understand? When there

is a calling over your life, nothing in hell can stop you, not even a disease that is known to kill people." Maxine squeezed my hand even tighter.

"God is trying to tell you something," she said. "Open your heart and your ears to Him and He will show or tell you what to do. You are His lamb and you will hear His voice in the name of Jesus. I pray that you hear him now, Tami, I really do. The rest is truly up to you." Maxine began to pray for me under her breath. I couldn't hear everything that she was saying but I didn't need to. I knew that it was no one but God who brought me to Maxine, so that she could minister to me. He allowed her to share her story with me and put me in line with how I was about to destroy everything I have worked so hard for. It's time for me to make up my mind if I will die without my purpose or live without my purpose. Those are the two roads that I am currently on. *I have to make a decision and make it quickly, because time waits for no one.*

Chapter Eighteen

I parked my Toyota behind Chris's car. I wasn't expecting him to be home. *Home? My home.* I took a deep breath and climbed up the stairs. Unsure of what was about to take place, I went ahead and put my spiritual armor on. I'm ready for war, ready to stand against whatever it was I may face in the next few minutes.

Chris greeted me at the door with a smile and a hug. "Hey baby, where you been?" He gave me a kiss and pulled me into the dining room.

I looked around and noticed there was a strange smell in the house. Like Chinese food or something. *I didn't cook,* I thought to myself.

"I ordered us some lunch. I figured that I should treat you to a little something since you have been working so hard these past of couple of days." Chris swiftly walked into the kitchen and brought me out a dish that had rice and sweet and sour chicken on it along with a glass of grape juice. He then ran back into the kitchen and brought his food and drink to the table.

He sat down, grinning from ear to ear. All I could do was look at him. He bought us lunch. He even put a nice cream colored silk tablecloth on the table. *He went all out for me.* I was flattered and appreciative, but I was still on the mission to get rid of him once and for all. *There is nothing in my mind that will keep me from finally getting rid of this poison that is hindering my life.*

"Um, Chris ... this is nice and all, but—" I started to speak, but Chris was very excited and beaming as if he had won a million dollars.

"Look, Tami baby, before we talk about anything else, I wanted to give you some great news."

"Oh? What's that?" I asked. The scent of the sweet and sour chicken was irritating my nose, although it did look delicious.

"I got another building signed on today!" Chris remained smiling, waiting for me to jump for joy, but I honestly had no idea what he was talking about.

"I don't understand …"

"Oh, sorry, I know this is business talk. I contracted another site today for my cleaning business. It's a building downtown, one of the high-rises." He pulls a brochure out of his pocket and hands it to me. He points to the building that he is referring to.

"It's one of the larger buildings downtown. You don't understand, this is big money, right now! More than double what I am making now with two smaller buildings!"

I looked at Chris. I had never seen him so excited. I was happy for him, but at the same time, my mind was ringing with things that I wanted to say to him.

"Chris, I really need to talk to you." I tried to talk, but he continued to interrupt me with all of his excitement. He was so happy that I could do nothing but just listen. He even brought up how he was so thankful that God was making a way for him to leave a legacy behind for his future family. I nodded in agreement and threw in a smile every once in a while. *What was he getting at with all of this?* I wondered.

Chris got quiet. I took it as an opportunity to get in what I had been trying to say to him. He took me by surprise when he got up from his chair and walked over to me. He grabbed my hands and stood me up, facing him. I could feel the rapid beating of his chest against mine. I was confused and yet comforted by his touch. His arms felt confident and strong against the middle of my back.

"I love you, Tami." The words burned into my ears. I can't remember the last time he told me that he loved me. My heart was racing and my eyes were searching for the room to be on fire or maybe I would wake up and I was in a dream.

"I said I love you, girl," Chris said tenderly. He rocked me side to side as if there was music only he could hear. I was still speechless.

What do I say? I asked myself. *I do love him, but, I couldn't get the words out right away.*

"I love you too, Chris," I responded softly, looking into his eyes.

He is everything that I want in a man. He has changed for the better, I told myself. *He can be a provider for me and our future children. He would go to*

church with me and pray with me in my time of need, wouldn't he? I suddenly couldn't remember what I desperately needed to talk to him about.

"I know this is sudden. I just had to let you know that I'm not afraid to tell you how I feel about you. This is real, the way I feel about you." He bent down and kissed me gently on my lips. "You're a great woman and I want to spend the rest of my life with you. I know I do."

My face became warm and my knees became weak. If my heart would beat any faster, I knew the next thing to come would be a heart attack. I realized that I had tuned Chris out for a moment.

"You can even quit your job, I'll take of you. I will, I promise. That is … if you feel the same way about me."

Chris searched me for a response. I had my mouth open to speak, but the words just didn't come out. I wasn't sure what to say. *What do I do, God? Is this of you?* I have been waiting for Chris to say those very words to me and now they are here. He said all the right things. *Marriage. Future. Love.* This was almost too good to be true.

As if the moment couldn't get any more intense, Chris goes into his pocket and pulls out a little light blue box. He takes my hand and places the box in the palm of my hand. I couldn't believe it; the box said Tiffany and Co. I knew it wasn't a ring. But it was Tiffany's! I opened the box, and to my surprise, there was a little locket in the shape of a heart with diamonds around it. It was the most beautiful piece of jewelry I had ever seen. He took it out and slipped it on my wrist.

"I know this is not the engagement ring I wanted to get you, but I hope you like it," Chris said, smiling, as he put it on my wrist.

"I do love it, I do. I don't know what to say." I could not take my eyes off this gorgeous piece of jewelry or this man who stood before me, so genuine and loving.

"I know this is sudden. I really do. But I have thought it through. I really want you to be my wife. I want to be with you. I know we have our differences, but I know that we can work through them. I'll do whatever it takes to make you happy, to make us work."

Chris spoke without taking a breath. I realized that I was also holding mine as well. I wished that I could freeze the moment and start my day all over again. I started out having every intention of kicking Chris out and moving on with my life, but I would have been miserable all over again. I would be lonely and feel like I was missing out on love again. I had to know if Chris was for real, because I had some demands to make. If he

was willing to uphold them, I was willing to be with him. I had to keep it that simple.

"Okay, Chris," I started out firmly. "This is a little sudden for me. I would be lying if I said that I didn't love you or have strong feelings for you. I would be lying if I said that I didn't want to marry you. I do want to. I do know that you would be a provider and a good man to me. I know all of this," I took a deep breath and continued. "But I need you to be sensitive to where I am in my relationship with God right now. I need you to know that we can't have sex anymore until we are married. I really mean it. Okay? Can you respect that?" *I made my point plain and simple.*

Chris nodded his head, and I was relieved. I told him how I felt and what I wanted. *You go, girl!*

"No, I need to hear that. Do you understand what I am saying to you?" I spoke firmly.

"I understand. I am willing to wait for you. I won't ask you for anything or touch you or try to change your mind. *None* of that. I respect your decision completely." Chris answered as he looked at me adoringly.

"Good. I need you to also make an effort to go to church with me. That's very important to me, because we have to grow together spiritually." I sighed and took a deep breath. Chris nodded in agreement and reminded me that he would do whatever it took to make me happy. *It was music to my ears! I was getting married to the finest, most wonderful man on earth. Thank you, God!*

Chapter Nineteen

The next four months seemed too good to be true. Chris actually upheld his promises to me, including a beautiful pear-cut diamond ring. The wedding was only two and a half months away, and there was still much to do. We finally met each other's families, and thank God my mother approved of him. It helped that he has been coming to church with me *faithfully* every Sunday. Maxine was also very supportive of our engagement, but not so much the living arrangements. I knew that she didn't approve of Chris and me living together before marriage, but she always kept her peace and accepted my offer to be my Maid of Honor.

I was also glad to be singing in the choir again. I love looking out at my future husband sitting out in the audience watching me bless the Lord with my spiritually gifted voice. Now I had the best of both worlds, and Chris was in the most important part of it. I could not have been any happier in my life. It seemed the days couldn't be going any faster. Even though I was able to quit my job and let Chris foot the bills, I thought that time would move slower, but it seemed like the days escaped ahead of me.

The more excited I was about the wedding, the more work seemed to need to be done. Maxine and I spent the days picking out items and having girl talk. I knew that deep inside, she wanted to say more to me about marrying Chris, but she respectfully kept her thoughts to herself, and I respected her for that. Most girls don't get the same chances in life, and when we do, we should embrace it! At least, that's my philosophy.

Chapter Twenty

The Sunday before the wedding, Chris decided to drop me off at the apartment early because he had to go back to the office. He invited me to go with him, but I decided to head on home and take care of house business and wedding stuff. We kissed each other goodbye and parted ways. I skipped up the stairs into my building and hummed on the way up to my door. I couldn't wait to look at my bridal dress. It was an egg white, heart-shaped dress with the longest train I have ever seen on a wedding dress!

I went over to my desk, which was originally the dining table, and checked off things to do on my wedding to-do list. Maxine finally got her dress together, and she loved the lavender dress we picked out together. Maxine had definitely been a great help to me for the past couple of months. I was truly grateful for her. Earlier today, she did ask me if I was having second thoughts, and I happily told her that I wasn't. She smiled and gave me a hug and said she was just checking. I know she wants the best for me. As for my mother and my aunts, they think I hit the jackpot with Chris. I always have to remind them that I was marrying for love and nothing else.

I decided to head out to get some take-out for dinner. I can't remember the last time I cooked at home. *I will cook something special tomorrow*, I said to myself. It was already after four o'clock, and Chris would be ready to eat when he got home. I changed clothes and headed down the stairs. When I got outside, I saw a woman standing beside my car and looking around as if she was impatiently waiting for someone.

"Are you waiting for someone?" I asked politely as I walked over to her. I would have thought she was a bum or something, but she was dressed neatly in a pair of fitted jeans and a long-sleeved shirt with Nikes. She was brown skinned and not that much taller than me, and she was really skinny. The woman looked at me up and down and shook her head. She continued looking up and down the road. I could tell that she was very irritated and getting impatient. I shrugged my shoulders and headed to the driver's-side door ready to hop in my ride.

"This your car?" the woman asked.

"Yeah, Why?" I asked calmly. She was really starting to trip me out, especially when she came around to where I was and stood in front of me.

"You know Chris?" she asked haughtily.

"Yes, I do he's my boy—I mean my fiancé." I held up my ring to show her.

"Yeah, I figured so. Your car is always parked behind his." The woman turned her back on me and started to walk away. *This girl is crazy*, I thought. *She been staking us out or something?* I wondered. The woman turned around and walked back toward me. I took a couple steps back and got on my guard, just in case she felt stupid enough to hit me. I was pretty sure I could take her.

"I don't have anything against you; I'm just looking for Chris." The woman spoke swiftly and kept her gaze on me. *Now, why in the hell was this trick looking for Chris?* I asked myself, suspiciously. My flesh was beginning to rise up. I had to keep my feelings under control. *Keep cool, stay saved*, I told myself.

"I don't—well, he went back to his office—" As I replied, she laughed and waved her hands at me.

"His *what? Office?*" She started laughing. "Okay, I see. That's a good one." She laughed some more, and I was beginning to be offended, but I kept my cool and let her talk. *I will loose my religion on her if I have to*, I wanted to slap her but I kept my cool. I needed to continue be a lady. I haven't been saved all my life, so she need to watch herself.

"Look, I just wanted him to know that Jaleel needs clothes for school and his tuition is due for his karate class. I just want the money, and I will be happy to leave him alone."

Jaleel. That name rang a bell in my mind. I just couldn't remember where I heard the name though.

"Jaleel?" I asked, confused. That name sounded very familiar.

"Yes, his son," the woman said smirking. *Ding, ding, ding. His son, that's right. Dang.* My heart sank first and then came the butterflies.

"I know you have it all good right now with Chris, but if you don't mind," she said sarcastically, "please remind him that he has a son who needs him too." The woman walked off and left me standing there bewildered. She turned back around and smirked at me. "Let him know that court is this Friday for the child support hearing, and he better show up this time."

The woman turned the corner, and a few moments later, I saw a white SUV speed off so fast that I heard the tires screech. *My God, what just happened?* I asked myself. *Jaleel? His son? Child support case? This Friday? The wedding is on Sunday.* Hundreds of thoughts flashed through my mind. I was still trying to recall the day that Chris almost broke down and cried over the heartache of finding out that Jaleel *wasn't* his. She had to be lying. *Or was Chris lying?* Wait, she knew my car and where he was living. So who was lying? *They must have spoken here before,* I thought to myself. But she has just never seen me, only my car.

I needed some kind of emotion right now. Was I angry, hurt, ashamed, or stupid? No, I had no feelings. None whatsoever. *Feelings about what?* A bitter ex-girlfriend mad because I have the ring she always wanted? *No,* I said to myself, *I shouldn't be thinking that way at all. For all I know, Chris could be lying.* But my bet is on Miss Mystery Lady, who appeared to be so brokenhearted because her baby needs money, poor thing. *Oh well.* I hopped into my car and carried on with my day like nothing happened. *Females are so desperate these days,* I thought to myself shaking my head.

Chapter Twenty-One

It was already Friday, and the week had gone by slowly. I wondered if Chris would mention something to me about this child support hearing that was *supposed* to be taking place. Naturally, he probably wouldn't since he already told me the kid wasn't his and that a DNA proved it. So what would be the need of a child support hearing then? The wheels in my head had been turning over and over the past few days. I hadn't seen the woman since the other day, and I found myself looking for her whenever I went outside. With the wedding almost a day and a half away, I began to get more curious about her. Chris acted normal all week. He was excited about the wedding and the bachelor party his friends were throwing for him. He is supposed to leave tonight, and I won't see him again until Sunday at the altar. *I have to act like nothing happened. I have to act like I don't know anything,* I reminded myself. *God, what shall I do?* I asked impatiently. I stood in silence, hoping to actually hear from God, but there was just silence.

"Tami, can you pack some extra shirts for me in my bag. I'm 'bout to roll out," Chris called from the bathroom.

"Sure." I packed his bag quickly. I decided that when he left, I would go ahead and make a few calls to see what was up with Chris and his *potentially* secret life. I wasn't ready to jump to conclusions yet. I needed a plan. *God, what should I do? What to do? What to do?* I thought eagerly to myself. Suddenly, I heard the voice of God whisper in my ear: "child support case." Today was supposed to the hearing! Chris was supposed to be there. I know for sure he never went to court, because he has been getting ready for the bachelor party and the wedding all morning. *Thank*

you, God. I know what to do. I'll take a trip to the courthouse in the hopes of running into Jaleel's mother.

Chris couldn't leave the house fast enough. I reassured him that I would see him on Sunday at the altar and that I loved him so much. We exchanged kisses and he gave me a wad of spending money for the weekend.

Chapter Twenty-Two

I drove Chris's car to the courthouse and parked in the front parking lot. I had no idea if the hearing was over with or not or if there even was a child support hearing to begin with. I decided to wait outside by the steps and look out for her, hoping and praying that she hadn't left yet or even showed up. If she was never here, that means there was no child support hearing, which also means that she was actually the one lying all along and not Chris.

I waited outside for what felt like hours. I was getting restless and hopeful at the same time that I wouldn't see her at all before the close of business today. *I was tempted to walk inside, but how would I know exactly to go? God, you led me here, now show me something. Anything.* I fed the meter a couple more quarters and walked down the sidewalk for hot dog and a soda. It was getting late and I was very hungry.

"What brings you out here?" A woman asked at the hot dog cart. She wore dark shades and had on a pantsuit. I assumed she was a lawyer or something.

"Oh, just grabbing a bite to eat," I replied nonchalantly as I placed my order.

"You don't remember me?" the woman asked, laughing.

I took a closer look at her, and this time she had her shades off. She looked a lot different. She had strikingly beautiful eyes, but I could tell they were weary with stress. She smiled and shook her head. *Dang. She was here.* My heart sank a little.

"Girl, I know you remember me. I certainly remember you, with that big ol' ring on your finger," she said, laughing some more. "I met you the other day."

I was so surprised to see her that I was suddenly shy. *Now what?* I asked myself. *I was actually hoping to not see her.* I thought to myself. I was definitely disappointed. All the fingers pointed to Chris that he was a liar. *I'm sure he has an explanation,* I told myself reluctantly.

"Yeah, of course, I remember you," I managed to say. I noticed the line was starting to get long after I got my food. She ushered me over to the side and we walked over to the benches.

"I'm Brenda, by the way." She introduced herself as she bit into her hot dog.

"Tami," I replied. We sat for a moment and said nothing. All I could hear was the mastication in my mouth.

"I don't suppose you spend a lot of time in court. You were looking for me I bet." Brenda spoke as if she was sure of herself, but she didn't make eye contact just then.

"You came here to find out if I was lying about Chris, didn't you?" Miss Brenda was smart. "You're starting to have questions about your man?" Brenda chuckled to herself and continued eating.

"Well, I just want to know the truth. I think that I am entitled to that," I said coolly. I didn't want her to think that she was intimidating me.

"Did you know that it's against the law to neglect a child and not pay child support?" Brenda got up and threw her garbage away in the trash can that was across from us.

"It's also against the law to have a co-signer for a brand-new car and not uphold your part of the contract to keep up with the payments." I could feel her eyes on me, watching me for a reaction. I decided to keep my cool and not let her get to me. *What was she trying to tell me?* Brenda apparently has some screws loose.

"What are you talking about?" I asked getting irritated now. I was trying very hard not to snap on this girl. "Look, I don't know you," I said. I decided to get straight to the point. "I guess that I just came here to see … I wanted to know if you were still seeing each other and if you were lying about Chris having a child support hearing." *I wished that I didn't come here. This was not my battle to fight. I had no business being here.*

"See? That's what's wrong with females these days," Brenda said angrily, "You think that just because I want Chris to start acknowledging his son that I want him back? I do feel sorry for you. I just want what's best for

Jaleel, that's all. Make no mistake, Chris *is* on child support and he *is* behind on his payments *and* the other obligations that we agreed to."

"So *is* Jaleel Chris's son?" I asked sarcastically. *Two can play this game.*

"Did he tell you that he wasn't?" Brenda retorted. She reached into her purse and pulled out her wallet.

"You tell me if that *is* Chris's son." She snatched out a picture and handed it to me. Brenda certainly was sure of herself and she was not backing down.

I looked at the picture and tried very hard not to find a resemblance in the features. Brenda seemed to have nothing to do with reproducing Jaleel; he was every bit of Chris, from the hairline all the way down to the chin. Jaleel even had Chris's smile. I remained numb for a moment.

"I know this is a lot for you. I would say that I'm sorry, but I'm not. Chris needs to step up and be a man, be a father. If he doesn't want to do that, I have to get the courts involved. Plus, he owes me money. I allowed that man to drain me for years until he finally got on his feet and decided that my son and I would be too burdensome." I could hear the hurt in her voice along with the anger and resentment as any woman would have. How could I have believed Chris's story and bought his sorry fake ass tears? I felt stupid, and I wanted a deeper explanation.

"When is the wedding?" Brenda asked curiously.

"Sunday," I whispered. I could hardly speak. I wanted to fall into a black hole and disappear.

"Congratulations. I really do mean it. Hopefully, he will do right by you. *Hopefully.* I use that term loosely. Once a dog, always a dog." Brenda and I met each other's gaze. For a moment, we understood the deceit we had both endured, by a man we have both given our heart to.

"I'm sorry, too. I really am. I had no idea." I had nothing else to say. I got what I came here for. I stood up and exhaled deeply. I guess I had been holding my breath the whole time.

"It's not your fault. Look, like I said, all I want is for him to acknowledge his son and pay me what he owes me. I could care less what else he wants to do with his life. As far as I'm concerned, he will need you to help him out every once in a while. I'm sure he won't be able to do it all alone on his salary."

"I'm not sure I understand what you mean." I went and stood in front of Brenda, facing her head on. "What are you saying?"

"Girl, you seem smart, but you lack common sense. I'm trying to tell you that since he didn't show up to court to face me, I'm having his checks garnished. That should catch me up for almost three years worth of child support he owes me." Brenda shrugged her shoulders and smirked.

"I know you may think I'm being vindictive, but I don't care. It's not about you or him. It's about my son. Between now and a few more months, he will have to answer to the government, and believe me they will seize his stuff—including that little fancy ring you got that I'm sure isn't paid off yet."

My mind spun a million times in a matter of seconds. She basically told me that Chris and I were about to be struggling because of the money that he owed her. Did Chris think that I was going to foot the bill for him and his past mistakes? Was he using me this whole time?

"Hey, will you need a ride home?" Brenda asked. I looked at her, baffled.

"No, I don't need a ride, I drove here," I replied.

"I think you're going to need a ride; they're towing your man's car." Sure enough, I looked over my shoulder, and the Acura was riding by on the back of a tow truck. I looked at Brenda with crossed eyes. Apparently, my eyes questioned if she had anything to do with the car being towed.

"Well, I guess this is starting sooner than I thought. They must have got it for nonpayment or the unpaid parking tickets he owes on it. Oh well, I would be happy to give you a ride home. I have to go that way to get Jaleel from the babysitter anyway."

Brenda and I rode to my house in silence. I was already humiliated that the car was towed and worst of all, Brenda was there to see it all happen. I could imagine her telling her friends about what happened or how stupid I was for not knowing how trifling Chris could be. How could I be so blind? No, I wasn't blind. I wasn't stupid, just exposed. Chris allowed me to be exposed to his mess. I felt let down and misled. He could have told me all of this from the beginning. Now here I am, taking a ride from his baby mama to get home because the car was towed due to his negligence. I had to plan my next move. The wedding was the day after next, and Chris and I still had some unexpected holes to patch up.

I was glad to finally get out of Brenda's car. I wanted her to have her time to chuckle and giggle to herself. But I was getting out of the car with dignity and nothing less.

"Thank you for the ride home," I managed to say without bursting into tears.

"No problem, girl. What are you going to do now?" she asked. I thought about it for a moment, and then I smiled the most genuine, personable smile ever.

"I'm going to go finish up the final touches on my wedding and get ready for the bachelorette party." I went into my purse and pulled out an invitation that I just *happened* to have in my purse. I handed it her and looked her square in the eyes.

"I would love for you and Jaleel to come to our wedding. Feel free to stop by the bachelorette party as well."

I felt good about inviting Brenda to the wedding. I didn't see any reason at all why she shouldn't be there.

Chapter Twenty-Three

Sunday morning came quickly. Maxine and the girls from choir threw a wonderful party for me Saturday night. I was all too pleased to have so much positive energy surrounding me on that day. It was truly a Saturday filled with lots of music, makeovers, and desserts. I felt bloated and nauseous. My nerves were in knots, and the butterflies in my stomach seemed to be competing for space.

Today was it, this was the day the Lord has made just for me. I was tempted to lie back in the bed and disappear into the sheets forever. In three more hours, I was to be the wife of a man who kept secrets from me, a man I did grow to love and fall in love with. I imagined us finally being able to make love. I couldn't wait for the moment to give myself to him as his wife. I looked at the pear-shaped diamond ring on my finger and smiled. I had to make the best of this day, no matter what, and nothing was going to get in my way of making sure that happened.

In the midst of my thoughts, a group of women burst through my door. Everyone was yelling at one time to get up and get dressed, get the makeup, get the hot curler, and make sure the flowers are right this time. Of course, my mother was the ringleader. Maxine found me in the middle of everyone and gave me a hug. She reminded me that she had been praying for me and that she loved me.

"Maxine, come help me figure out this train on this dress. I don't know why y'all get something so long and complicated. Come on, ladies, hurry up! The limo will be here in an hour and y'all still look a mess in here!" My mother must have planned to continue shouting and giving orders all the way to the church. Surprisingly, my head wasn't ringing with all her

demands and shouting. The other ladies shrieked with excitement as I was finally a finished product to walk down the aisle.

"You ladies ready to go?" My mother asked shouting. Everyone shouted their reply and we headed out the door. As we were walking out, Brenda was standing at the elevator.

"Hey, Brenda! I didn't know you were here!" I exclaimed. I was truly surprised that she even came. I wasn't sure if she would actually show up.

"Are you sure it's okay for me to be here?" She asked nervously as the other women were staring at her.

"Yeah, I am. Where is Jaleel?" I asked. "I hope you brought him."

"Oh yeah, he is in the car with my mother downstairs. I just wasn't sure…"

"You're fine, Brenda. I'm glad you came. Really," I replied tenderly.

"Who is this, Tami?" My mother interrupted, she was obviously confused.

"Oh, I'm sorry, guys, for being so rude. This is Brenda, the mother of Chris's son, Jaleel." The hallway remained quiet for the first time in minutes. Finally, Maxine came forward and gave Brenda a hug.

"Well, it's nice to meet you, Brenda." Maxine ushered the other ladies to say hello.

"I guess I'll see you at the reception?" I asked Brenda. She nodded her head and smiled at me. *She really is a nice girl.* I thought to myself. *Today is going to be a good day. I was trying not to smile because I knew my mother was watching me closely.* I caught my gaze of bewilderment. It was her first time even hearing about Jaleel or Brenda.

Chapter Twenty-Four

The ride to the church was long and drawn out, with lots of questions about who Brenda and Jaleel were. I was sure to answer some questions—but not all the questions. I didn't want to make a bigger deal out of the situation than it was.

I was in the back of the church when I heard my cue to start waltzing down the aisle. I said a prayer before I went out there. My pastor stood in to walk me down the aisle since my father was deceased. I was glad to have him there with me for support and spiritual connection. My knees were buckling as I went down the aisle. I was holding onto my pastor as tightly as possible for balance. I figured I could pass out at any moment. The church was bigger than I thought. I could see Chris from a distance, beaming from ear to ear in his white-and-lavender tuxedo. He looked strikingly handsome. I wondered silently to myself if he spotted Brenda and his son among the guests in the pews.

I looked for Brenda and noticed her sitting in the back on the side. I briefly noticed a young boy sitting next to her, and an older woman *who I already knew to be her mother*. It seemed like I still had twenty feet to go until I reached the altar. The lights were so bright that I felt perspiration under my arms. Luckily, I was wearing a powder deodorant so I was protected from sweat stains (or so I hoped).

I finally made it to the altar, where my future husband stood waiting for me so patiently. I could tell that Chris was admiring how beautiful I looked because he did not take his eyes off of me for a second. The pastor gave me a kiss on the cheek and sent me into the hands of the man I had waited for all my life. His touch made me tingle all over, and I couldn't

take my eyes off him either. Chris looked so fine in his white and black tuxedo. He looked like a million bucks. I searched him to see if there was any doubt in my mind that he did love me. I searched him to see if this was a man God approved of being in my life. *What a fine time to think about this,* I said to myself. I tried to not smile at the thought of God standing over the ceremony with a lightning bolt, ready to strike at any moment.

The preacher was speaking about how God made man to be with a woman, and how a man who finds a wife finds a good thing. Chris was listening closely, nodding his head and laughing at the preacher's jokes. I had tuned the preacher out long ago as I began to think about my journey with Chris, and how I wasn't sure about our relationship or *him* for that matter. I caught Maxine's gaze, and I knew that she was watching me. She had been praying for months about the wedding. I recalled to my memory that a few weeks ago Maxine told me that no matter what, God's will would be done. *Isn't that the truth?* I said to myself sarcastically. The preacher asked us to prepare our vows. Chris's uncle, who was his best man, handed him a card. Chris cleared his throat and took my right hand and held it in his hand firmly. He found my eyes and looked into them deeply.

"Tami Monique Simmons, I stand before you today, not as a perfect man, but as a man. I intend and desire to be your man forever. I desire to be that man you can depend on and that man you can trust. Through thick and thin, and of course, till death do us part." Chris closed the card and handed it back to his uncle. I can't say that I was floored by his vows, but I did applaud his effort. The first thing I noticed was what he *didn't* include in his vows. I realized that I was expecting him to include God in his vows, because that meant he would be including Him in our lives. It was my turn to say my vows and I had them memorized from the heart. I waited all weekend to say my vows to him, and now I finally had my chance.

"Christopher Harper Brennen, you are truly a man who had captured my heart. I never thought I could ever fall in love with the man of my dreams. For so long, I waited for God to send me a man who would be honest with me, love me, and cherish me the way you do. I prayed for you and fasted for you for so long. Now that you are here, I plan to love myself the way that I love you, most of all, I plan to love God the way I love you. But now I'm not sure that I can continue to allow myself to love you anymore." As soon as I said that, I heard loud gasps and whispering in the audience. But I needed to keep going. I have to say what is on my heart no matter what.

"I wanted to love you forever and ever until death did us part. That's what I intended to do before I found out who you really were." More loud gasps were in the audience. Chris' face continued to be stiff as stone. Everyone at the altar seemed to be clearing their throat at the same time.

"Now I know that I want a man to love me the way that God loves me. I don't want a man that I love before God and myself." Now people were whispering among themselves a little louder. Chris' face continued to be stiffened as if he were a corpse.

"I also want a man to love his children as well. The Bible says that a man who doesn't take care of his children is equivalent to an unbeliever. I believe, Christopher Harper Brennen, that you are an unbeliever, because you are not a man who cares about his child. I wouldn't want to marry a man who doesn't love or acknowledge his children." I decided to ignore the whispers and gasping. I had to keep on going because I was on a roll. *Can't stop now.*

"I'm sorry, Chris, but I cannot compromise who I am for you anymore. Yes, I love you. Yes, I want to be with you, but I cannot be with a man who tells lies and hurts people. I cannot be married to a man who isn't first married to his responsibilities and God. I pray that you forgive me, but most of all, I pray that you make amends with your son and his mother. You have put them through a lot of unfair treatment. Your son is handsome; he looks just like you. You have the opportunity today to see your son and tell him that you love him. They're sitting right there in the back on the right-hand side. They came as my guests, but now they are leaving as my friends." The whole congregation seemed to be looking over their shoulder to the back of the church, even the preacher. My job was done.

I wiped a single tear that reached the top of my cheek. There was no need for it to fall any further. I gave Chris the tenderest kiss on the cheek that I could give him. He remained silent and stunned. I went to the back of the church and found Brenda. I took the engagement ring off, grabbed her hand, and placed the ring in it, gently.

"This belongs to you, Brenda. It should help catch you up with the car payments, tickets, and everything else Chris owes. Pawn it, sell it, wear it, whatever you want. Apparently, the ring was paid for in full." Brenda smiled at me and I winked back at her. Behind me, there were more gasps and whispers. I didn't bother to look back as I walked out of the church and into the cool air that I longed for.

Why Not Today?

Is there a time limit on love and forgiveness when a whole family is torn apart by one person's selfish decisions?

Chapter One

It's too hot for Darla to walk to her interview, so she decides to catch the bus. She swats at the sweat that's dripping down her forehead over her well-groomed bangs that are now matted down with moisture. Darla sighs in frustration as she realizes that she must have dropped her handkerchief on the way to the bus stop. She takes off her shoes and looks down at her feet. Darla notices that they were swollen from the heat and from the shoes being a size too small. She thinks to herself that she should have gotten the larger size of the black soft-soled shoes she saw. But the brown ones were on sale and she would have rather saved two dollars than buy her right size in shoes. Darla was always a woman of shortcuts, who believed in the saying: "Work smarter, not harder." Of course, she understands now that if she wanted to get anywhere in life, she should think of a more effective motto to live by. She hasn't thought of one yet because she is too busy thinking about her daughter Isabelle, the daughter who probably doesn't even remember her.

Darla began to wonder what she looks like now. Is she tall like her father now? Does she have long hair or short hair? Is it curly like her father's? She hasn't seen her daughter since she was nine years old. Darla knew that she made a lot of bad choices in her life. She basically chose men, alcohol, and drugs over her family.

Although Darla had a handsome husband who treated her like gold, a wonderful child, and above average wealth; through therapy and rehabilitation, she came to the realization that she had been using drugs and other "irresponsible behavior" to fill the emptiness that she felt in her life.

Darla and Henry had Isabelle two years into their marriage. She loved her daughter, but at some point, she got tired of her marriage and tired of being a mother. Finding other men in bars and clubs gave her a rise in her life. She loved the adrenaline rush that she got when she would take a chance on leaving the bar with a strange man to find out what new drug she could try or what combination of liquor would get her drunk faster.

Darla remembers the last night her and Henry argued before she decided to finally leave her family for good. Henry pleaded with her and even cried in front of her. He attempted to unpack her suitcase as he begged her not to leave and to think about what she was doing to Isabelle. Darla remembered vividly Henry telling her that he was willing to do anything to make the marriage work and that he would pay for rehab and a family counselor to help her with the demons she was battling. She recalled laughing at him and telling him not to worry about her anymore because he will probably find someone else and forget all about her. Just as if the scene was playing in her mind all over again, she could hear Henry's voice in her head. He looked at her with longing, loving eyes as he said: "I will never find another woman like you. I only want to be with you, Darla. *Please, please* don't leave. Don't tear this family apart."

There was nothing that Henry or anyone could say to her, Darla decided to walk out on her family and live her life the way that she wanted to. It didn't take long for Darla to sink deeper and deeper into a dangerous lifestyle.

Chapter Two

Darla didn't have to go far into her memory as she recalled living with boyfriends who preferred to beat her with closed fists. Prostitution came quickly when she needed to make a quick dollar for food and rent. There was no way she would work a nine-to-five when she could make her rent money and utilities in two days. Drinking Bacardi and Belvedere straight every morning for breakfast and before bedtime helped with numbing the fact that she was selling not only her body but her soul for money. Then, after the liquor couldn't numb her anymore, it was cocaine who became her source of comfort. Within just a few months, Darla was getting high more during the day instead of prostituting. She eventually lost her apartment and became homeless.

Darla had given up on herself until one day a tall Hispanic woman in a navy blue dress suit saw her sitting outside of the Port Authority. She handed Darla a pamphlet with information about applying for a free therapy and rehabilitation program. The woman informed Darla that the program was funded by a grant and that the funds were limited. She didn't waste time to see if Darla was interested in the program. Her job was done and it was up to Darla if she wanted to do anything with the information that she had just received. Darla watched the woman as she walked off and handed another pamphlet to the hobo that was sitting by the doorway of the Port Authority begging for money. She watched the woman walk across the street until she disappeared out of sight. Darla decided it was time to make a change in her life and she was determined to act quickly to save her spot in the program.

Darla was able to get into the program and within one year and six months she was sober and drug free. Her therapy was helpful because she was able to discuss her feelings and find the root of her poor decision making over the years. Upon completing the program, she was also super happy to find out that she had a clean bill of health after her first physical was completed. To her surprise she was disease free. After years of drugs, alcoholism, and some nights of unprotected sex with strangers, she managed to only have a urinary tract infection at the time of her physical. Darla asked God for forgiveness for her years of disobedience and thanked Him most of all for protecting her from everything and everyone that could have had the chance to kill her.

Her counselor was kind enough to set her up with a boarding room until she could get her a job and her own apartment. The last thing on her list to accomplish was to find Henry and Isabelle. Darla was willing to do whatever it took to make that happen. It has been at least ten years since Darla walked out on them. Would they even consider taking her back?

Chapter Three

Darla takes a well-deserved seat at the bus stop. She still has less than ten minutes for the next bus to come. Darla went all out to get ready for this job interview. She found a great outfit and a pair of shoes at the Goodwill for next to nothing. Darla even rehearsed in the mirror how she would answer her questions at the interview. She would sit up straight, smile, speak clearly, and be personable. Darla straightened her hair and curled her bangs. She put on mascara because it made her brown eyes pop out a little bit to give her more of a "youthful" look. Despite everything that she has been through the last decade, at thirty-seven, she didn't look too bad compared to the other women that she was in the program with who were younger than her.

Darla is "conventionally" pretty, as society would put it nicely. She is tall and full-figured, neither too skinny nor too plump. Her hair wasn't very nappy, but straightening would do for now, until she could afford to get perms on a regular basis. Darla didn't have much to show for her life, but she was willing to work hard to get somewhere. She always found a way to get by without having to spend money on outrageous things.

The outfit Darla was wearing to the interview was a part of her "good clothes" collection. Basically, these were clothes she finds in the Goodwill bins that no one wants. She was able to find a long black skirt and a short-sleeved, cream-colored silk shirt to wear to the interview. She was proud that she was able to get a decent looking inexpensive outfit to wear because she was determined to make a great first impression.

God has truly blessed her with this job opening. There was no way she wasn't getting the housekeeping position at the hospital. She prayed and

fasted for two days so that God would give her some kind of favor. It's not a glamorous job, but at least it would get her started somewhere. Darla chuckles to herself that going to church really has helped to build her faith. She thought to herself happily: *Church is my lucky charm. Everything seems to go so right when I go to church.* Just then, the bus pulls up. Looking down at her watch, she sees that the bus is a few minutes early.

Chapter Four

As Darla walked into the building for her interview, she felt a burst of confidence and peace. She was able to catch a quick glance of herself in a mirror as she walked down the hall to the check in desk. The receptionist was talking on the phone when Darla approached the desk. She stood back a little so that receptionist wouldn't feel like she was hovering. She took a quick glance at the receptionist and admired how professional she looked. Her hair was very thick, long, dark, and curly. Darla could tell that the receptionist used starch on her clothes because it was ironed to a crisp. The receptionist was smiling into the phone and being courteous to the person on the other line. "We are here for you if you need us. Is there anything else I can assist you with today?" she asked politely. "It was my pleasure speaking with you today. Have a nice day." Darla came to the conclusion that the receptionist must be Hispanic because of her accent.

Immediately, Darla worried about her own customer service skills. Could she deal with people like that in a professional way? *She just has the extra energy to be that nice,* Darla thinks to herself. *I know I don't have patience like that.* The receptionist put the phone down and turned to Darla. She was smiling sincerely, and Darla noticed how white her teeth were. She became self conscience as she realized her teeth were nowhere near as white as hers.

"Can I help you?" she asked politely, smiling. Darla looked on the desk and saw that the nameplate said: Yissel Francorosario-Hernandez. *Yup, she was Hispanic, for sure, She thought to herself.*

"Yes, I am here for an interview with Mrs. Patterson." Darla tried not to sound nervous. Yissel smiled, nodded her head and began to type on

the keyboard. When she found what she was looking for, she grabbed a piece of paper wrote on it, and gave it to Darla.

"This paper shows you how to find Mrs. Patterson's office. This place is kind of a maze. Just follow the directions and you won't get lost, I promise."

Yissel chuckled. The instructions were simple: make two lefts, a right, a left, go all the way down the hall, and her office was the last one on the right.

"Thank you, you're very good at your job," Darla said, smiling.

"Thank you! Good luck!"

Darla nodded her head and waved good bye as she headed off to her interview.

Chapter Five

Darla was glad that she got there early, because it was a bit of a walk to get to Mrs. Patterson's office. Darla wished she wasn't dampened in her sweat and that she had on bigger shoes. *No more short cuts, it's time to work harder now,* she said to herself. Darla took a deep breath and knocked on the door. Her heart skips a beat and suddenly her stomach feels it has like a million butterflies in it.

"Come on in." The warm voice behind the door sounded inviting and polite. Darla felt a little better about facing the person who was going to be interviewing her. She said a quick prayer for favor and courage.

"Hello, it is so nice to finally meet you." Darla smiled as she spoke. She wondered if she sounded too fake or said too much already. Darla was struck by Mrs. Patterson's beauty. She appeared to be tall behind her desk. She was slim, with the brightest red hair she had ever seen. Darla wondered if that was her real hair color. *It couldn't be,* she thought to herself.

Mrs. Patterson was smiling at Darla. She seemed to be a friendly and genuine person. Mrs. Patterson stood up quickly and walked to the front of her desk to shake her hand. Darla noticed that Mrs. Patterson was wearing a black silk blouse with a khaki dress pants and black stilettos. Darla admired how professional and model-like she looked and wished that she had some of Mrs. Patterson's wardrobe, but in her own size of course. Darla chuckled to herself at her silly thought while she shook her hand and took a seat in front of the desk. She observed Mrs. Patterson closely as she flipped through some papers. When she found the right one, she gazed at Darla intensely.

"I reviewed your application, and I saw that you didn't have any experience with hospital housekeeping."

Darla was somewhat startled by Mrs. Patterson's statement. As friendly as she was, this wasn't the opening she was hoping for.

"I didn't see on your application that you even had any documented work experience," she continued. Mrs. Patterson looked at her as if she was waiting for a reply. Darla was lost for words. What could she say? Maybe being quiet was the best thing right now.

"What makes you think you would be a good asset here at Parkson Hospital?" Mrs. Patterson finally asked. Darla cleared her throat and chose her words carefully just like she did when she rehearsed in front of the mirror.

"Well, I believe I would be a great asset to this hospital because I am responsible, I want to work *harder*, not *smarter*, and I am willing to learn anything."

Darla was quite impressed with herself because she remembered the key words she needed to use in order to impress Mrs. Patterson. She didn't know that she could articulate that well. At least, she hoped she did.

Mrs. Patterson seemed unmoved. The expression on her friendly face was blank. "Without any work experience, how do you know you will do well?"

"Well ..." Darla didn't know where she was going to go with her reply; she decided to just go with the flow and answer the question. "I know I would do well here because I am willing to learn and I am willing to work hard and commit to the challenges that will be placed before me." *Good job! Great answer!* Darla thought to herself, happily.

Mrs. Patterson clasped her hands together on her desk and leaned toward Darla with a serious look on her face. "I am wondering what exactly you did all these years if you were not working."

Mrs. Patterson was looking into Darla's eyes as if she was trying to see if she was willing to lie. Darla didn't know which way she should answer the question, and she figured that she may as well be honest with her.

"I must say that I am ashamed to even tell you. But I know that in order for me to able to work here, I need to be honest from the start. I have been in a rehabilitation program for almost two years. Before I enrolled in the program, I was a junkie and a prostitute until I became homeless. Before I was a prostitute, I was a wife and mother who decided to leave her family to run wild and live dangerously. Now I am ready to get on my feet and start working so that I can get back on track with my life."

Darla realized she was talking with her eyes closed. She opened her eyes slowly and saw Mrs. Patterson leaning back in her chair, tapping her pen on her desk. Darla looked down at her feet, and she could feel them throbbing. She was ready to get on the bus and go home. *Well, the truth will make you free,* Darla reminded herself sadly.

"Well, quite a story," Mrs. Patterson said. "I do believe that you would be an asset in the housekeeping department."

Darla was shocked; she thought her eyes were going to pop out of her head. *What did she just say?* Darla wanted to run around the room screaming and shouting, but she managed to compose herself.

"I want to start you out on a trial basis for a month. If you prove to me that you can handle the work, I will hire you on full time with Sundays off in rotation with the other employees." Mrs. Patterson clasped her hands together and smiled. It was obvious that she admired Darla and the story that she had behind her.

"Oh, thank you, Lord!" Darla exclaimed.

"I want you to tell me something and be honest with me," Mrs. Patterson said seriously and quietly. "How long have you been clean and sober?" she asked, curiously.

Darla looked at her and smiled proudly. "Almost two years." Darla was proud of her sobriety and wasn't too ashamed to talk to people about it or to tell other people about her past.

"Well, I have been sober for almost five years myself. Isn't it a great feeling?"

Mrs. Patterson? Sober? What? Darla thought surprisingly. Wow, she didn't know she was talking to a recovering alcoholic!

Darla was trying to stay calm. "Congratulations! I know you are very proud of yourself."

"Yes, I am, and congratulations to you too. I look forward to working with you. I am willing to give you a chance. Unlike other people I have been interviewing, you're not just looking for a job, you're looking for a chance to make your life better, and those are the kind of workers that I need on my floor. Welcome aboard."

Mrs. Patterson's words stung Darla like a bee, and she thought she was sweating again when she tasted water at the side of her mouth, but it was really her tears streaming down her face.

"You start next Monday morning at eight o'clock sharp; don't be late."

Darla nods her head and smiles. She murmurs: "Thank you," as she turns around and heads for the door. Darla couldn't be more proud of herself. For the first time in her life, Darla felt like she had a chance to make her life better.

Chapter Six

Darla walked out of the hospital and caught the bus that had just pulled up. She was so relieved to sit down and pull her heels out of her shoes to let her feet stop throbbing. The whole way back to the boarding house, Darla was rejoicing and thanking God for her second chance at a new life. She couldn't wait to get off the bus and tell her friend about the job she just got.

Darla became good friends with Linda while they were in the rehabilitation program together. They were both able to convince their counselors to let them become roommates in the boarding house because they had become so close that they didn't want to be separated right away.

Linda was a woman who ran away from her abusive husband. The very first time Darla saw her; she was bruised and beaten up, with blood and scratches covering most of her face. Linda was shorter and more slender than Darla. She was in her late twenties, with brown skin and curly, dark hair that was attributed to having a white mother and black father. Her eyes were almond-shaped, and had dazzling brown irises that sparkled when she laughed or smiled. Linda's face healed after a few months and Darla was able to see her face without the cuts and bruises, she noticed that Linda was a beautiful woman.

Linda had a deep scar around her neck from when her former husband tried to kill her by cutting her throat. Linda called the scar her war wound and evidence of being a true survivor.

She told Darla the horrible story about the night she tried to leave her husband, or at least what she remembered. He had beaten her so much that she blacked out.

Linda had finally found the courage to leave her abusive husband. Derrick tried to convince her to stay and promised that he would never put his hands on her again. Linda spit in his face and told him to go to hell and that she was done for good this time. She ran into the room to pack her bags, and suddenly she felt Derrick grab her from behind by her hair and began beating on the back of her head with his fist and then threw her on the floor and began kicking her in the back with his steel-toed work boots. That was when she blacked out after the pain was too much.

Linda woke up staring into the blade of his pocket knife. She recalled to Darla how she felt the knife draw across her skin on her neck. Linda was lucky that the knife missed the artery in her neck by a mere half of an inch.

Linda was sitting outside of the building, on the top of the stairs. Her hair was pulled back, and she had makeup on. Darla noticed that she was wearing her new white button-up shirt and black dress pants. She looked at Linda, puzzled, wondering why she was dressed up.

Darla greeted Linda cheerfully. "Hey, girl, what are you doing out here? Why are you all dressed up this afternoon?"

Linda smiled at Darla. "What? I can't dress up in nice clothes every once in a while?"

"So no special occasion?" Darla asked laughing.

"Well, no, not really, I just had lunch with a friend today that's all," Linda smiled. Darla knew that sparkle in her eyes was hiding something.

"*Oh really?* A friend? Who? Do I know him?" Darla asked as she walked up the stairs and took a seat next to Linda.

"No, you don't know him, he is just a friend. *Nothing else.* What about *you?* What's with the fancy outfit?"

"Well, since you want to change the subject about your new boyfriend;" Darla said jokingly. "You won't believe what happened to me today!" Darla exclaimed with wide eyes, gleaming with anxiousness to tell Linda about her day.

"Girl, what is it?" Linda asked smiling.

"I finally got a job!" Linda squealed and hugged Darla tightly.

"What did you expect, Darla, to *never* ever get a job or something?" Darla put her finger on her chin as if she was really thinking about it.

At some point, she was discouraged, but at the same time, she never lost faith.

"Well, girl, with my past luck, I wasn't so sure. I start working at the hospital on Monday!"

"I'm so happy for you, I really am." The good friends embraced each other again.

"The only thing left to do is find my daughter and Henry." Her excitement made her forget about the swelling of her feet. Darla sighs, kicks off her shoes and puts her head in her hands.

"I do believe I know where they are. Knowing Henry, they probably never moved. I just have to get there and see how they receive me or *if* they will receive me." A tear falls onto Darla's wrist. Linda pats Darla on her back to console her.

"Darla, you have come too far to be feeling sorry for yourself now. You don't have time for that. Go find your family. Go to them and ask for forgiveness. That's *all* you can do. There is nothing else to do, you know that." Darla wipes her eyes and stands up.

"You're right, Linda. I have a few days until I start work. I can catch the train to get to the city and see if they are still at the same house. What could it hurt?" Darla said feeling more hopeful than before. "I'll leave in the morning to get an early start." Darla gets up and goes inside the building.

Linda called after her. "Where are you going?"

"To pack." Darla disappears through the door and went upstairs to her room. She was excited about the day she was going to have to tomorrow. Sure, she was nervous, but her excitement let her forget about her nervousness altogether.

Chapter Seven

Darla woke up the next morning feeling light-headed and nauseated. All the excitement she had felt the night before now felt like fear and doubt. She pulled the covers back and walked slowly to the bathroom. Darla saw herself in the bathroom mirror. The reflection staring back at her was the woman she was ten years ago. The woman back then was thinner, her long hair was past her shoulders, her makeup was flawless, and she had a look on her face that seemed to read "sexy confidence." Now the woman standing before her was older and chubbier. She had a small scar on the top of her left eyebrow from a bar fight she was in. Her hair was a little shorter, and her complexion was blotchy.

Darla smiled at her reflection. It was a forced smile. She was trying to convince herself that no matter what, she *was* beautiful. She grabbed her toothbrush and toothpaste and started brushing her teeth. Darla had already laid her clothes out on the bed. She quickly got dressed in her khaki pants and brown dress shirt. Today, she wanted to be comfortable but not look like she was living in a boarding house. This time, she was going to wear her flat black leathers shoes so that she could walk all day if she needed to without feeling like her feet were on fire.

She carefully combed her hair back into a ponytail and put on eyeliner and lip gloss. She didn't want to overdo it. *A little goes along way,* she thought. Darla smiled in the mirror again, and this time, she was fully convinced that she was more than beautiful. She gathered her bags, and as she was opening the door, Linda spoke.

"You're leaving already, Darla?" Linda yawned and sat up on the bed.

"Yeah, I have to get an early start." Darla walks over to Linda's bed and gives her a hug. "I'll call you from a payphone when I get there and tell you what's going on."

"I know you will find them, I know you will." Linda squeezes Darla and ushers her out of the door.

"Hurry, hurry, hurry, you won't want to miss the first train."

"It's only a twenty-minute ride; I'll be fine. I love you and I will be in touch." Darla hugged her friend and headed out of the door.

Darla walked out of the building and caught the bus to the train station. She got there about ten minutes early. She sat down on a bench and decided to pray until her train came.

"Lord, I know that I don't deserve this blessing, the blessing of being able to find my family. But I know that you are a God who sits high and looks low. I know that you know my heart because you are God. I pray that you guide me on this journey for forgiveness. I pray also that if they don't receive me or forgive me right away, I pray in Jesus' name that in due time, they will. Amen."

Darla was meditating for a while, and then she heard the train come. She hurried on and took her seat in the back where she would be sitting alone. The nervousness kicked in again. In twenty minutes, she was going to be "home." Darla immediately changed the way she said that in her mind. *No, not home, just to my family, my husband and my daughter.*

A tear streamed down her face, and she quickly wiped it away. She began to fill her mind with positive things to think about. Darla began to think about what she would do and what she would say. She realized she hadn't even bothered to look them up in the phone book because she would rather be rejected in person. At least she would be able to see them and at least they would get to see her.

Chapter Eight

The train ride ended quickly. *That twenty minutes felt more like twenty seconds*, she thought to herself. It was nine thirty in the morning, and the sun seemed to be beaming right on her. She got off the train and went into the ticket building where she sat down a bench to think about her next move. Darla wondered if she should walk, take the bus, or catch a cab. *Is it in vain to go all the way to go to the house where she left them?* Darla asked herself. If she knew Henry like she thought she did, he didn't sell the house and move. Henry hated moving. He had always told her that where they settled is where they would be. No changing jobs and moving around. Henry hated change.

Darla was his first and only girlfriend. They met in middle school and went steady all throughout high school. Darla knew that Henry had eyes for no one else. He was the most handsome man at school, tall with awesome curls in his hair. His complexion was always flawless, and his smile was riveting. Darla remembered the first time she saw his chest. It had no hair, and that turned her on. Instantly, she didn't want to be with anyone else, and she certainly didn't want him to be with anyone else. Henry was very loving and caring. He was a good man and a great father.

Darla's friends used to envy her, because Henry, who was a contractor, would buy Darla cars and mink coats. When Isabelle was born, she had more toys and dollhouses than the toy store. Darla felt herself getting angry and frustrated. How could she let all that go? Who in their right mind would do that? She realized that was just it: she wasn't in her right mind. When Darla finally got the therapy she needed, she was diagnosed with

depression. Depression? Darla remembered chuckling out loud when the therapist told her that.

"You mean I left my family because I'm *sad?*"

"Well, a lot of people in your position use 'adventures' to cover up their sadness so that they won't have to deal with the reality of their sadness and repressed issues." Darla remembers being puzzled and angry at the therapist. *Who was she to judge how she was feeling?*

"Darla, think about it," the therapist said. "You were beautiful and young and outgoing. You fell in love at a young age, had the perfect family, the perfect dream. But you realized that it wasn't yours. It was all your husbands' You were feeling inadequate. You made up in your mind that your life was boring and that your family didn't deserve you. You would rather leave them than have them leave you. You practically thought your life was too good to be true."

Looking back on what on the therapist said, some of it now made sense. Either way, what she did was wrong and now she was ready to make things right.

Darla grabbed her bags and walked to the taxi stand. She was ready to get a move on.

Darla didn't hesitate as she instructed the cab to take her to 57 Sumner Street.

Her heart was beating too fast, and then she began to wonder if Henry remarried. Darla convinced herself that he must have, and she needed to be prepared for that. *I wonder how pretty she is. Is she treating Isabelle right?* She thought to herself, sadly.

"Miss, you said 57?" The driver interrupted Darla in the midst of her thoughts. She looked around at her surroundings and saw that nothing had changed on the street. The houses were the same; the trees were the same. She hadn't noticed the rest of the town because she couldn't concentrate to pay attention. She rolled the window down and recognized the scent of freshly cut grass.

"Is this the right house, miss?" the driver asked.

"Oh yes, yes it is." Darla fumbled around for her bags. When she looked up, she saw the driver staring at her in the rearview mirror. She noticed that he was Indian. *He speaks good English,* she observed.

Darla looked at the house and saw that it was the same, a three-story brick house. It was one of the bigger houses on the block. She remembers there being only two other black families on their street. The shutters were black, and she noticed a flower garden in the well-kept front yard. *Oh yes,*

Henry is definitely married, because I know that he doesn't garden or know anything about flowers for that matter. Darla sighed deeply and felt the pang of discouragement.

"Do you want me to wait for you?" the driver asked.

Darla thought that would be a good idea, since she wasn't sure anyone was home or if they would just slam the door in her face. She noticed a car in the driveway. It was a pretty new-looking car, a black Acura. *It had to be Henry's,* she concluded. *He loves black cars.* She knew he was home or at least his wife was there.

"Yeah, please. I will only be a minute, I promise. Oh, what do I owe you?"

The driver glanced at the meter. "Fifteen seventy-five. The first five minutes free, and after that, it's a dollar every two minutes."

Darla hands him exact change and grabbed her belongings.

"Don't worry, I won't leave. I will be right here; just give me a signal if you need me to leave."

Darla nods her head and makes her way across the street slowly. Darla's heart beats so fast that she could feel the pulse all the way in her brain, it seemed. She looked back at the cab; it wasn't too late to turn around and forget the whole thing. *No, no, I need to do this.*

It seemed like it was the longest walk ever. She couldn't feel her pulse anymore. She felt numb. Darla got to the door. It was painted a pale yellow color. *It used to be black. I guess Henry decided to change the door color, or maybe his wife did,* she said to herself. She put her two small bags on the floor and pushed the doorbell nervously. As soon as she pushed it, she heard it ring through the door. Darla heard footsteps coming to toward the door quickly. She closed her eyes and found herself bracing for shock.

"Hello? Can I help you?" Darla heard the voice of a woman and slowly opened her eyes.

The woman standing at the doorway was tall and beautiful. She had a short haircut and wore a yellow dress with white flowers on it. Darla noticed that the woman was well-accessorized with white hoop earrings, white bangles, and white baby doll shoes.

"Can I help you?" the woman asked again. Her voice was soft and polite. Darla didn't know what to say or how to answer. Henry's wife was beautiful. Darla instantly became insecure and wanted to leave. Of course he was married. Why wouldn't he be?

"Ma'am?" The woman asked waiting for Darla to answer.

Darla snapped out of her trance when she heard footsteps and a man's voice.

"Who is it, sweetheart?" The man came closer to the door. Darla was trying not to gaze at him. She was trying to recognize him. But she already knew it was Henry. *He said: "sweetheart,"* Darla thought sadly. *He's married.* Henry seemed to not have aged at all. He was still lean and slender, and he had a goatee now. His curls were cut off into a low hair cut, and his voice was still the sound of the sweetest love song.

"Can we help-" The man's voice stopped at the middle of sentence.

He stared at Darla, and she stared back at him. The woman in the yellow dress stared at the both of them, looking back and forth. It seemed like everyone was frozen for an eternity. No one moved; no one said a word.

Darla realized that all she was hearing was the sound of a bird chirping and a car driving by. She looked behind her, and the cab was gone. Darla turned back around and stared into the eyes of the man she had left ten years ago. He looked puzzled and confused. Maybe there was some anger in his eyes, but Darla swore she saw joy and surprise—but she wasn't sure.

"Do you know her?" the woman asked.

Henry stepped forward and met Darla on the top step outside. He came close to her as if to make sure that she was real. Darla still had not spoken a word. Her muscles were tight and her eyes were burning, as she was fighting back tears. She knew that if he came any closer, she would be even more tempted to grab a hold of him and just squeeze him. But she didn't want to make a spectacle of herself in front of his wife.

"Yes, I know her," Henry whispered softly. Darla just stood there. The words were right there on her tongue, but she couldn't get them out. What should she say first?

"Who is she? Is she okay?" The woman seemed genuinely concerned. She was looking over Henry's shoulder, to understand why they were staring at each other so strangely.

"Isabelle, this is your mother," Henry said softly.

The woman looked at Darla with puzzled eyes and Darla put her hand on her chest and began to sob immediately. She looked at Isabelle, confused. *Isabelle? Forgive me.* Her eyes looked at Isabelle as if she could read her thoughts. Darla broke down and fell to her knees. Sorrow, relief, and joy were all the mixtures of emotions that Darla felt at the same time.

Henry reached down and hugged Darla while she was on the floor sobbing. He embraced ever so gently and whispered softly to her that he couldn't believe it was her. Isabelle stood in the background still shocked at what was taking place before her eyes.

Chapter Nine

Henry grabbed the bags and took Darla inside the house. Isabelle followed behind them at a distance, still not understanding what was going on. As they walked into the house, Darla noticed that everything in the house was the same, except for the furniture. Isabelle handed her mother a box of tissues and watched Darla dry off her face and blow her nose as they sat in the kitchen. Henry and Isabelle were staring at Darla as though she had appeared from the grave.

"I guess I should be saying something," Darla started. "The truth is that I don't know what to say."

Henry and Isabelle appeared to be looking for Darla to say more, so she continued slowly. "I'm sorry I ran out on you guys. I'm sorry I didn't write or call. I just wanted—"

Henry raised his hand to interrupt Darla. He spoke gently, "Look, Darla, I know that you're sorry, I know that you were troubled back then. But you are here now, and I know my prayers have been answered. I am only thankful that you are here and that you have decided to come back to find us and to seek forgiveness."

What? Darla couldn't believe what she was hearing. Her heart was pounding and her stomach had those butterflies again. It felt like she was on a really fast roller coaster ride.

"I would like your forgiveness," Darla said. "But I know that I don't deserve it." Tears began to fall down her face. Darla took a tissue and began to wipe them away quickly. Darla saw that Isabelle was staring at her.

"I always wondered what you looked like," Isabelle said. "I couldn't remember your face for a long time," she said gently.

Isabelle had tears welling up in her own eyes. For the first time in ten years, Darla hugged her daughter. Darla couldn't help but sob again, louder and louder. She repeated how sorry she was, over and over again. It seemed like she said it a million times.

After the two women finished sobbing and hugging each other, Henry walked over to Darla and took her hands into his. Darla was so afraid to look into his eyes that Henry took her chin and lifted her head to meet his gaze.

"Both Isabelle and I have prayed for this day for many years. It has been hard without you. There were many nights when I said I hated you. But I asked for forgiveness, and in my asking for forgiveness, I forgave you. We forgive you, Darla. We don't have to talk about the past. Although it will take some time to warm up each other, we would like to first start with breakfast. Will you join us?" Darla looked deep into Henry's eyes and saw the love that she had for him in there. If her heart was made of butter it would have melted from Henry's gentle touch.

"Yes, of course, I would love to," Darla replied. Isabelle took her by the hand and sat her down at the kitchen table.

Over breakfast, they chatted and laughed. Isabelle told Darla that she was finishing her third semester of college at Michigan State University, majoring in Biology. Darla beamed at her daughter. She was a beautiful young lady who had grown into a lovely flower.

"Henry, are you still in contracting?" Darla asked.

"Oh yes, the business has expanded and things are going great. What are you doing now, career-wise?"

Darla told them about working odd jobs and volunteering in the community in exchange for a room at a boarding house until she got on her feet. She proudly told them that she got a job at the hospital and was planning to get her own place in a few months.

"How long will you be here for?" Isabelle asked.

"Well, I have to be at work on Monday, so maybe I can get a hotel and come see you tomorrow and leave on Sunday."

"Nonsense, there is a guest room upstairs. You can stay in there if you would like," Henry offered.

Darla smiled and looked at Isabelle for approval. Isabelle gave her the thumbs-up sign and nodded her head. Darla happily accepted the offer.

All her dreams were coming true. Darla got her family back. After ten years of being away, she felt like she had never left them. *Why today?* Darla

pondered. *Why today and not five years earlier or even ten years later? I guess everything does happen in Gods timing, in His season.* Darla smiled. She was okay with God's timing for everything. Today was just fine for her. *Why not today?*

Why Not Today?
Part II

Chapter One

I woke up the next morning and realized that I was in the guest room of my former house. I recapped in my mind all the events that took place the day before. I still couldn't believe how well everything went with both Isabelle and Henry. I sat up on the bed and looked around. I don't remember too much about the guest room, because I rarely used it. The wallpaper was new, and the room smelled a little of paint, like it was renewed recently. The walls were a beige color, and the wallpaper that lined the top of ceiling was of burgundy flowers. I do remember the room being carpeted before, but now it was polished wood. I got off the bed and walked over to the oversized dresser. It was cherry wood, and so was the queen-size bed; nice touch. I love the cream-colored silk bed sheets; it made me think of the fancy and expensive bed comforters that you see in the upscale home magazines.

I wondered what Henry was doing and where Isabelle may be. Despite the good night we all had together, laughing and talking, I was feeling a little shy to leave the room without fixing myself up. I went over to the window, and I saw that Henry was digging around in the garden in the front yard. I would never imagine in a million years that Henry would be gardening. He was on his knees, digging back and forth, back and forth in a slow motion. He stopped for a moment to dry the sweat on his forehead. I could see his white T-shirt sticking to his back and that's when I noticed his muscular frame. The muscles in his back seemed to be dancing around in his shirt. Henry kneeled back down in the dirt, and for some reason I was feeling my heart pounding in my chest, yearning to wrap my arms around him and to rub my hands up and down and around his muscles.

I immediately canceled that thought out of my mind because I knew he had to have a girlfriend or a fiancé maybe. I didn't want to get my hopes up. But why would he want me anyway after ten years?

I remember the night I left I ran down the road and got into the car with my lover, Danny. He was one of the men I was cheating on Henry with. He wasn't as fine as Henry, but he was still a looker to me. He was short and skinny with a Jheri curl and one gold tooth in the front. I loved Danny's personality because he was a "bad boy." At the time, he was fun and adventurous. I remember going out to bars and getting drunk with him and then having wild sex afterward on the balcony of our hotel room.

We even stole outfits from a clothing store and wore them out to the clubs, showing off like we had it big. Danny was also the first person I tried marijuana with. The first time I got high with him; I was livid. The feeling of invisibility became addictive and I didn't have a care in the world. After my first high, my old life didn't matter anymore. I was finally living for me.

I decided to move in with Danny only a week after I left home. I was comfortable living with Danny in the beginning of our relationship because I liked that Danny ignored me sometimes as though I wasn't living in the same house with him. He gave me the space I needed to party as late as I wanted and smoke as much as I wanted to. I didn't have to work and I wasn't broke either. I was so used to Henry being all over me and telling me that he loved me all day long and somehow all that good treatment got old to me. Danny only told me he loved me when we were in bed together, and I didn't mind that because I wasn't looking for love. I was looking for excitement and adventure.

I don't know what happened after I decided to leave Danny and move on to someone else. I probably got tired of him. It wasn't hard for me to leave him because he never paid any attention to me and besides I didn't love Danny; I loved Henry. *No, I still love Henry.* I secretly wanted him back, but what if he didn't want me back?

Chapter Two

I went into my bag and pulled out my brown sundress. I have a feeling it will be hot today. I gelled my hair neatly back into a bun. I threw on a little bit of eyeliner and foundation with a touch of lip gloss. I don't normally use foundation, but I wanted to look extra good today for Isabelle and Henry especially. After another quick glance in the mirror, I was satisfied with the results. Just as I turned around, I saw Isabelle standing at the doorway of the bedroom. I almost didn't recognize her because she was dressed casually in shorts and a T-shirt.

"Good morning," Isabelle said smoothly still standing at the doorway.

"Good morning, Isabelle. How are you this morning?" I asked smiling at her. I wanted to hug her but I wasn't sure if it was okay for me to give her one or not.

"I'm fine," she replied. I got the feeling that Isabelle wanted to say more, but she didn't.

"Is anything wrong?" I asked, concerned.

"No, nothing is wrong. You look nice this morning." Isabelle looked at me up and down and nodded her head in approval.

"Well thank you. I'm still learning how to use makeup though," I laughed.

Isabelle still hadn't moved from where she was standing. I had a sinking sensation in my stomach that maybe something was wrong.

"I have a feeling that's not all you wanted to say. What's on your mind exactly?" I asked, bluntly.

I was relieved when Isabelle came into the room and sat down on the bed Indian style. I sat next to her on the edge of the bed, facing her.

"It's just that, I guess I should tell you that my dad didn't date much when you were gone." Isabelle looked at me with eyes that had question marks in them. I myself felt a little ping of happiness that Henry never *really* dated. I wonder if it's possible that he may still have a little bit of feelings left for me.

"Well, I'm not too sure why he wouldn't have dated. Your father's a handsome man. I'm sure he had his eye on someone, don't you think?" I was trying my hardest to be casual and not too nosy at the same time. I didn't want to give Isabelle the impression right away that I still had feelings for her father.

"See, that's the thing. While you were gone all these years, it seems like hundreds of women have tried to be with my father, but he was just *never* interested. I really think he couldn't move on all these years because he was still in love with you." Isabelle seemed to finally exhale. I noticed her watching me for an expression or a reaction to her statement.

How do I respond to that? What could I say? What should I do? Leap for joy? Spill the beans that I am still in love with her father and I was hoping that he would still give me a chance? At least I do know that he never moved on and that there isn't anyone else. I came to the conclusion that either he is gay, scarred forever by the fact that I left him suddenly, *or* he is still in love with me. I'm leaning toward the last two.

"Are you still in love with Dad?" Isabelle asked. I really didn't want to tell her right away that I was. At the same time, I didn't want to just ignore the question or lie.

"I have always loved your father, and I still do." *Bravo, Darla, good answer!*

"So are you still in love with him or not? I heard that loving someone and being in love with someone are two different things." Isabelle obviously wasn't happy with my response. She certainly knew a lot more about love than I thought she did.

"Yes, I am still in love with your father," I answered. *There I said it, bring out the judges!*

"I hope you do get to stick around, because I want to see you and Dad happy." Isabelle took a deep breath and continued. "I'm hoping that you guys can rekindle your flame because it would be a dream come true if the both of you were to get back together." With that being said, Isabelle jumped off the bed and walked out of the bedroom.

Chapter Three

After a few minutes of letting my talk with Isabelle marinate in my mind, I went downstairs for breakfast. Henry was in the kitchen already, making pancakes. He had changed into a striped short-sleeve shirt and jean shorts. He turned around when he heard me and jumped a little.

"You startled me! I almost forgot you were here for a moment." He chuckled and flipped a pancake over.

"Sorry about that. How has your morning been?" I wished that I had something better to say, but I didn't.

"Pretty good, thanks. Pancakes?"

"Yes, please," I replied. It was silent in the kitchen for a few seconds. It was an awkward moment with each of us wishing the other had something to say. I watched Henry flip and pat the pancakes in the pan, hoping that he would turn around and say something to me—anything.

"Orange juice or apple juice?" *Good. He asked me something. That kind of broke the ice a little bit.*

"Mmm ... apple juice, please," I said. I never really liked orange juice. Henry must have forgotten that about me.

"Yeah, I remember you never really liked orange juice; you would always drink either apple juice or grape juice." Henry smiled and turned to me, handing me the glass of apple juice and a plate of IHOP-style fluffy pancakes. I was happy that he *did* remember that about me. I found myself blushing like a little school girl. I tried to occupy myself by looking busy with carefully pouring the syrup onto the pancakes, making sure I didn't

miss a spot. Henry put his omelet on his plate and poured himself a cup of tea.

"You were always so strategic about how you placed your syrup on your pancakes." Henry sat down across from me and took a sip of his tea. He never cared for pancakes; he only made them because Isabelle and I loved the way he made them. *What a man!* I looked up at Henry, and he was staring right at me. I quickly looked back down at the plate and started cutting at the pancakes. I could still feel his gaze on me. I wanted to look up at him too and meet his eyes, but I knew that I am just not that bold. *At least not right now.*

"You seem to still have a lot of memories of me," I said. I really wanted to tell him how much I love him and that I wanted to be with him forever and ever.

"Don't you?" he asked me. *Of course I do. I have plenty of memories of you Henry. I wanted to express myself to Henry, but for some reason, I'm so shy. I wish I was bold enough to say what I really feel and what I'm really thinking.*

"Of course I do. I remember every once in a while you would surprise me with breakfast in bed." I looked at Henry and he was smiling. *That may have been too deep.* I wasn't sure if it was appropriate for me to bring up a "bedroom scene" just yet.

"What else do you remember about us, Darla?" Henry's voice almost sounded seductive to me. It could just be my imagination though. *It probably isn't!* I certainly hoped that it wasn't! I felt like he was trying to trap me to say something, but I just didn't know what it was. What could I say? I was still a little timid around him. *I need to loosen up.*

"I remember mostly the good times. Laughter, singing to each other, the love ..." I stuffed my face with a forkful of pancakes. I needed a moment to see where this was going. I grabbed the glass and drank as much as I could. I wondered if he could hear me gulping. *How much time can I kill to think of something else to say?*

"I still love you, Darla," Henry said softly.

What? My stomach felt heavy all of a sudden. *Love? Me? How? Why?*

"You do?" I asked him. "How can you still love me, Henry? Shouldn't you be angry with me?" I whispered. I was trying to catch my breath. It seemed like I was holding my breath unknowingly.

"Let's make something clear: I was never really angry with you, just disappointed. I knew that you had to battle your demons on your own; there was nothing that I could do for you." Henry continued to keep his

gaze on me. I wanted to run across the table and kiss my husband on the lips with all the love that I had inside of me for him.

"I love you because I know who you are and I love who you are. Nothing more, nothing less. I have to be honest with you. I still do love you, Darla." Henry continued to look at me and I met his gaze finally and kept it there.

"Well then, I have to be honest with you, Henry. I still love *you*. I always have. I was so afraid that you hated me and that you wouldn't let me back into your life, that you wouldn't forgive me for what I did to you and Isabelle." I lost my appetite suddenly. I couldn't even look at Henry anymore.

I was relieved, though, that I was able to tell him how I felt. I was convicting myself, and I knew that was an open door for my emotions to take over me.

"Darla, no one is perfect. You were dealing with demons back then, and I thank God that you have overcome them. I always knew that you would." Henry paused and took a deep breath. It seemed as though he too was fighting back tears.

"Although it was hard for me to lose you for a while, I had to realize that things happen for a reason. I'm not too sure what that reason may be exactly, to be honest with you, but I know that God doesn't make mistakes."

"Henry, I really feel like I don't deserve your love. I don't deserve a chance with Isabelle either." I pleaded with him. "I just want to know that your serious about me and how I feel." I finally let my emotions take over me. The tears I was holding back seemed to all come at one time.

"Stop right there." Henry slapped his hand down on the table; he got up from his chair and walked over to me. He grabbed me by the hand and stood me up in front of him. My heart was beating. *Was he about to kiss me?* I didn't want him to. I mean, I did want him to, but I didn't want our first kiss to be sticky with syrup. I looked at Henry and realized how true his love was for me. His clear brown eyes seemed so peaceful. I actually saw forgiveness in them, and I knew that he did really forgive me. It felt unreal, and the power of his touch was the most beautiful thing I had felt in a long time. I didn't want to talk; I didn't want to breathe. *I love you Henry.* I said to myself. *I love you so much. I love Isabelle too. I want us to be a family again.* I didn't have the guts to say those things out loud so I just stayed silent and enjoyed our closeness.

"I want you back, Darla," Henry said. *Did he say what I think he said? He wants me back?*

"I love you, Darla. I want us to be a family again." *What is happening right now? Was I talking or was Henry talking? What was he saying to me?* My knees were trembling, and I just wanted to sit down and think. *Think about what, dummy?* I asked myself. *He wants you back!* Everything I ever wanted to happen was unraveling so quickly. I guess it's true when God moves; He doesn't need to take his time!

Henry continued to speak. His voice was very deep and calm. It sounded like he was whispering a secret that he didn't want anyone to hear.

"I know this is all sudden for you. But I'm taking a leap here, hoping that you will accept us back into your life permanently. I don't want to live the rest of my life without you, Darla. My darling Darla," Henry continued to speak softly.

My insides were fluttering, and my heart had never beaten so fast. Henry was squeezing my hand harder and harder. *I just want to kiss him. I want to kiss him so badly.*

"We will take it slow at first, of course. I want to make sure that you are comfortable and everything." *This has to be a dream! Dummy, say something! What is wrong with you? Answer him, say something! Anything!*

I sighed deeply and took a breath. I honestly had no idea what I was going to say. "What about Isabelle? What will she think about this?" That's all I could come up with for right now.

"Isabelle would want nothing more than to see me happy; to see *us* happy. She leaves to go back to campus tomorrow, so it will be just the two of us. We will have time to get to know each other again and start fresh."

"Is it that simple?" I asked.

"It can be if you want it to be," Henry stared at me. I knew he was waiting for a reply.

"I- I- just got a new job … the boarding house …" My mind was racing so fast; there was so much I had to think about. *Everything was happening so fast.*

"I know. I thought about all that. You can decline your job and move here. I can get you a job at the hospital over here if you would like. I know some people that can get you in. You can stay in the guest room for as long as you like *or* we can share a room. Whatever will make you comfortable."

This whole conversation was going in a direction I only imagined in my dreams. I would have to give up everything to move back here into the home I know. I would have a better job, a good home, a family for once. *Should I give up everything to come back to Henry? I love him, I want to be with him, but do I love him enough to just drop everything and move here right away? Hell, yes!*

"Henry I would love nothing more in the world than to spend the rest of my life with you and Isabelle. I love you, Henry. I always have and I always will." I felt like the world beneath me was opening and everything was being sucked in except for two of us.

It was as if we were the only two people left here on Earth for a moment. Before I knew it, Henry leaned down and his lips were touching mine. They were still so soft and cold. I never understood why his lips were always cold. I loved that the most about them, because I began to warm his lips with mine. He opened his mouth and let his tongue gently into my mouth, and I let his tongue dance around my mouth with mine. I had forgotten all about the taste of syrup and pancakes in my mouth. I didn't even care; for all I know, it made the kiss sweeter. My body was tingling all over and chills were going up and down my back. I have a feeling that I won't be in the guest room for a long time.

Chapter Four

We finally pulled away from each other after a few minutes, but we were still holding hands. My eyes were closed for so long that when I opened them, the light in the kitchen made me see little green shadows and purple dots. What a kiss!

Isabelle suddenly popped into the kitchen with a puzzled look on her face. She looked back and forth to her father and then to me. "What's going on?" she asked. Clearly she was confused.

Henry cleared his throat and began to explain. "Isabelle, honey, I have some great news. Your mother and I are starting over." Henry and I were smiling, and he had his arm around me. I was waiting for Isabelle to jump for joy and squeal in delight. Instead she just looked at us.

"Well, this is kind of sudden. What about your job and your place and stuff like that?" she asked.

"We know it's sudden, and we are going to take it slow for now. But we are very confident that this is a good move, since we love each other and you very much. I'm giving up the job and my room and moving here permanently," I explained.

Isabelle's face didn't move an inch. No smile, no expression. *Nothing.*

I was both surprised and delighted when she ran over and hugged the both of us tightly. My heart melted when I saw that she was sniffling; I knew that she was crying. "This is a dream come true. I am so happy. I really want you guys to work out. I know you will." Isabelle stopped sobbing and kissed us both on the cheek.

I was touched by how genuine she was. I was also relieved that she received the news so well. She didn't seem to mind that everything was

happening so quickly. I couldn't be happier; I got my family back, for good this time.

Later on in the evening, I told Henry that I had to leave to head back to the city to pack up a few things. He offered to drive me instead of taking a cab. While we drove there, we listened to the radio and sang along together with the songs that we knew. He mentioned that a few of his friends from work were having a little gathering at the park and he wanted me to come with him. I was hesitant about that, because I wasn't sure what everyone knew about me, and I was afraid to face other people, especially his close circle of friends.

"Would you like to go with me? I think it would be fun," Henry suggested. He seemed to be excited about taking me around people he was close to. I was glad to know that he wasn't embarrassed by me, but I was still uncomfortable.

"I just don't know, Henry. What will people say?" I asked.

"Say about what?" he asked, confused.

"About us being together." I was a little bit frustrated. I wasn't ready to face people yet. I guess I may be a little ashamed or something. People's opinions don't really matter and I can't stop people from having them, but people can still be cruel.

"Look, I'm grown, you're grown. People can say what they want to say, but at the end of the day, the only opinion that matters is *our* opinion. Don't worry about them; let me worry about them." He grabbed my hand and kissed it. I was reassured that I shouldn't have to worry about what others may think. I have my family now, and no one can take that away from me.

We pulled up to the boarding house, and I noticed Henry's facial expression. He looked like he was wondering if I really lived there. I have to admit, the building isn't in the best neighborhood, and it isn't the best-looking building.

The boarding house building looks kind of like an old factory building from the early 1900s. It also has some missing windows that had wooden boards nailed over them and graffiti was also all over the building on the inside and the outside. It wasn't the best place in the world, but it *was* a home to me. Never in a million years did I think that I would be moving back to my old house with my husband and daughter. I was so excited to find Linda and tell her. *I sure hope that she is home.*

I told Henry to stay by his car and that I wouldn't be long, because I only had clothes and a few shoes that I owned. I really just wanted to

gossip privately with Linda about the miraculous things that took place overnight.

I opened to the door to my room, and Linda was sitting there on her bed, reading a book. She jumped up when she saw me and gave me a hug.

"Girl, I thought you said you were going to call me!" I know that she was more excited to hear what happened than she was to actually see me. I couldn't stop smiling, and I truly didn't know where to start my story.

"Well? How did everything go? What are you smiling for? What happened?" Linda was asking a million and one questions.

"Linda, you wouldn't believe what happened." Linda beckoned me to keep going and hurry up. I laughed.

"Henry and I are back together." Why prolong it? I went ahead and gave it to her straight. The expression on her face was priceless. Her jaw dropped and her eyes got wide.

"Isabelle and I get along great. She is in college, tall, and beautiful, and she is so thrilled that her father and I are back together. Of course, we are taking it slow, but eventually things will get on track for us."

"Darla! *Are you serious?*" Linda obviously couldn't believe the news; she put her arm over her mouth and squealed. "Oh my gosh, Darla! I am so happy for you! So where is he living, was he in the same house or what?"

"Yeah, he never moved or been with any other women. Can you believe that? He also wants me to move in and everything." As soon as I said that, Linda's face dropped. I could tell that she was sad. I was so caught up in my own happiness that I didn't even consider the fact that she would really miss our friendship.

"When are you moving in?" she asked sadly.

"Right now."

"Now! Are you serious? What about the job you got?" Linda asked. She started pacing back and forth.

"What if it doesn't work out, then what? Are you ready to give up everything for him?"

"Linda, I thought about all of this already," I said defensively.

"I'm ready for my true happiness with my family. He has a few links at a nearby hospital. I can start right after I get settled in. It's not like we are sleeping together right away. I will have the guest room until we are more comfortable with each other, of course. We love each other, and that's all that matters."

I went to the closet and started packing my things as fast as I could. I was a little bit disappointed in Linda's response. I didn't feel like hearing any negativity.

"Darla, I *only* want what's best for you. I don't want you to be hurt or anything." Linda sounded apologetic, and I knew that she was just looking out for me; that's what we did for each other. I zipped up the bag with all my stuff and put my bag at the door.

"Are you taking the train back there or something?" Linda asked.

"No, Henry is downstairs waiting for me in the front."

Linda ran to the window and looked down. "I know that is not him down there by the black car." I looked out the window beside her, and there Henry was, waiting patiently, leaning against the driver's door with his foot across the other one. He looked so good in his dark blue khaki pants and button-up white shirt that he changed into for the party. I was proud to show him off for a moment.

Linda looked at me and rolled her eyes. "*Girl,* you don't plan on being in the guest room for long, do you?" We laughed and gave each other a high five.

"I would leave this dump, too, Darla; go get your man!" Linda and I hugged and promised to be in touch with each other. I gave her my new address and told her I would never forget her. I took my bag and happily went to go meet my man downstairs.

Chapter Five

As soon as we left the boarding house, we drove for ten minutes in the opposite direction, to the park where his co-workers and friends were having a party. I was still a little uneasy, but I was glad that I was dressed in my sundress for the occasion. Henry parked the car and came around to open my door for me. *What a gentleman he was!* He took me by the hand, and we walked slowly into the park. Off in the distance, I could see at least fifteen to twenty people there already. I have to admit that I was a little nervous, but at the same time, I felt good knowing that Henry was holding my hand and supporting me being there with him.

As we walked up a little closer to the party, I noticed people poking at each other and whispering, looking in our direction. My stomach had butterflies in it again. I think Henry could sense my nervousness, because he squeezed my hand a little, and when I looked at him, he winked and smiled at me.

While we were approaching slowly, a tall, preppy-looking white man with a pale yellow vest and white shirt walked up and greeted us politely.

"Hello there, Henry. Glad you could make it."

They shook hands, and Henry introduced me. "This is Darla. Darla, this is Frank. He's my right-hand man when I need something done the right way at work." The two men chuckled and then Frank's gaze to turned to me.

"Well, this is new, Henry. You never bring a date to these things," Frank looked at me and smiled. "You must be a lucky lady to be here with Henry."

Two more people overheard Frank talking and came over to greet me. The uneasiness went away for a second. I was surprised at how friendly people were being. I wondered what their motives were. I noticed through the crowd of people talking that there was a black woman sitting off by herself, scowling at me. Or at least I thought she was.

The day at the park was going really well. I was glad that people assumed that Henry and I were "dating"; I guess that may be a good word for us. Although we never technically got divorced, it's almost as if we were engaged again.

I excused myself and went to the bathroom. It was a little dark, and I had to find the light switch. I eventually found the switch after palming around on the bathroom wall. I tinkled, washed my hands, and then started to re-apply my lip gloss and eyeliner. I didn't look bad; my bun was still intact and my hair was still gelled down to perfection. I smiled in the mirror because I was pleased with a day gone well so far.

I guess I was so busy looking at myself in the mirror that I didn't even notice that the woman that I saw earlier was in the bathroom with me. She was looking at me through the mirror at my reflection. Her hands were crossed at her chest, and she had the same scowl on her face. I started to turn around and politely ask her what her problem was but instead I smiled at her and asked her how she was doing. She didn't answer me; she walked to the sink next to mine and continued to stare at me. I was really about to lose my patience with her.

"I'm sorry, do I know you?" I asked. I was trying to remain as classy as possible. I wasn't about to pull my bun down for anybody.

"So I guess your Henry's girl, huh?" The woman turned the water on and began to wash her hands.

"I guess so," I said smoothly. *Who is this lady?* I asked myself. I didn't owe her any explanation. I didn't know who she was or if she was even that important to know. I packed up my little makeup and began to walk out. I turned back to her for one last word. I told her to enjoy the rest of her evening and I went out the door.

I was proud of myself for not going "negro" on her. If this had happened ten years ago, I might have slapped her or worse. Instead, I was a lady about it, and I was proud of myself. I decided that I wouldn't tell Henry what happened in the bathroom because I didn't want to worry him.

I was flattered that someone took the time to make an unpleasant face at me. I found Henry in the crowd of people and went up to him and grabbed hold of his arm.

I heard someone ask Henry, "When did you guys meet?"

Henry spoke proudly and I started blushing a little bit. "Well, Darla and I have known each other for years," Henry stated. "She's my wife, actually." The crowd suddenly got silent, and all I could hear for a moment were the birds chirping off in the distance. *I always seem to hear birds when there is silence.* I didn't expect Henry to spill the beans so soon to his friends about us.

"*Really?* Darla's your *wife?* I didn't even know you were married!" Frank exclaimed laughing.

"I thought I knew everything about you, but I guess I don't!" Henry and Frank laughed and a few of the spectators joined in with them.

"Yes, well, we were actually separated for a time, and now we are working things out and getting back together." Henry explained after he finished laughing at his friend. I noticed a few people nodding their heads indicating that they understood his explanation.

I got the impression that Henry respected our privacy. Everyone doesn't necessarily have to know the *whole* story. I couldn't wait to get back home. *Home.* It sounded so lovely just to have that to say. Home for me used to be a little room with chipped blue paint, a constantly broken toilet, hard mattress bed, roaches, rats, and a microwave. I was thankful for the boarding house. It kept me safe and off the streets, but now I had a husband and a daughter. A family, *my* family.

Right now, this was all a dream that I can't even conceive mentally. *Everything was going so right suddenly, how can this be a reality?* I felt Henry's warm hand on the small of my back as he leaned down to my ear and whispered, "Are you ready to go now?" I looked at him and nodded my head.

We waved good-bye to everyone, and at the corner of my eye, I noticed the woman from the bathroom staring at me again. I waved to her anyway and walked off with Henry. I wasn't the least bit worried about her. Where I am going, she won't be there, so it really didn't matter.

"Did you enjoy your time tonight?" Henry asked me gently as he opened the car door for me.

"Yes, I must say that I did. Your co-workers were very polite to me."

"They're good people. I try to come to these gatherings to get to know everyone; it keeps us motivated at work. You know, it boosts morale when everyone gets along like a family," I nodded in agreement.

Chapter Six

Family has become very important to me because I didn't really have one when I was growing up. I was an only child whose mother was a depressed alcoholic who turned tricks every once in a while to cover whatever bill was past due that month. My mother, Lona was the person in my life who disappointed me the most because she was a college graduate who practically let gin and orange juice ruin her life.

I used to look at her pictures and try to imagine being as beautiful as she was. I remember seeing a picture of her in her early twenties. Her jet black hair was straightened neatly with a part in the middle. Her hair was so long that it fell past her shoulders. Lona's eyes were bright, full of hope and a bright future.

My mother always told me never to value any man higher than I value myself or God. She contradicted herself when her hopes and dreams were shattered by a drug dealer she fell in love with named Maxy. He was the man who got my mother pregnant and disappeared. He was also the man that Mother loved and the man that my grandmother Nana Mary hated. I recall hearing my grandmother talking to my mother about him when I was a little girl. Nana Mary hated my father, apparently because he abandoned my mother and me. As a child, I remember wondering, how could he have abandoned me if he was never around to begin with?

Before Nana Mary died, on her deathbed she made me promise to always value family no matter what happens in life. She squeezed my hand with hers and made me look into her red, dying eyes. Nana Mary made me promise and I told her yes. Part of my pain in life was feeling like I let my grandmother down by not keeping the promise I made to her when I left

Henry and Isabelle behind. For years, I felt like my father's child, making a family and then abandoning them.

Lona was the first woman in our family to graduate from high school and Nana Mary was so proud of her oldest daughter because she went off to college and came out with her teaching degree. After my mother got pregnant out of wedlock my grandmother disowned her. After years of not being able to salvage the relationship with Nana Mary, my mother made alcohol and depression *her* mother figure. I knew that part of my mother's anger and pain was from disappointing Nana Mary when she was alive. Three months after my high school graduation, I found my mother dead on the living room floor; she finally drank herself to death. I figured that she died doing what she loved more than me.

When I married Henry after Lona died, I thought I would forget about my childhood and the bad memories that haunted me in my sleep and even when I was awake. My life with Henry was great in the beginning because I had everything that I could ever want; cars, clothes, jewelry, a big house, and money. I was rich and living the life that my Nana Mary wanted for my mother. I had the life that my mother would have envied if she was alive. I guess that's why she had to pass away when she did. It's sad to say but I'm sure that my mother would rather be dead then to see me happy and wealthy.

Chapter Seven

I found myself looking at Henry and admiring how wonderful he was. It still felt like I was living in a dream and I certainly didn't want to wake up. I wanted to stay in this moment with him forever. "What are you thinking about over there? You're mighty quiet. That's not like you," he said, laughing. "You seem to be lost in thought."

"Are you trying to say that I talk too much?" I asked jokingly.

Henry always had a strange sense of humor. I remembered the night he proposed to me. It wasn't a romantic proposal or anything like that. He simply said: "We should get married. Want to?" Henry smiled at me and tried to kiss me. I playfully pushed him away from me and he grabbed my elbow.

"What, you don't think I'm serious? Don't you want to have a million kids with me?" he asked, seriously.

"Why do you want to marry me, Henry? There is nothing special about me," I said huffing.

"Well, see, that's why I want to marry you." I shoved him hard in his chest, and he laughed at me. I knew he was joking. I figured if we could laugh together for the rest of our lives, I should marry him.

I shrugged my shoulders and answered him, "Why not? No one else will ask me."

"Good. It's done. I own you now." Without another word, he kissed me tenderly and promised me that he would take care of me and love me no matter what. I believed him. Even though I broke my end of the bargain, it's amazing that Henry still loved me after all I put him through.

I wished my mother could have made the wedding. But I also know that even if she did make the wedding, she would not have been exactly happy for me anyhow. I realized that my pain and reason for running away had a lot to do with the sadness I was feeling about the death of my mother and the broken promise that I made to my grandmother. I always wished that my mother loved me more; I wished all the time that I would have kept my promise to my grandmother.

"What are you thinking about now? Man, you are in deep thought tonight. Anything you want to talk about?"

"No," I answered shrugging my shoulders. "I was just thinking about the past, the good times and the bad times."

"Oh *yeah*, the good times." He turned the radio up a little bit more and began to sing to the oldies tunes that were playing. We sang along with the 70's greatest hits and enjoyed each other during the ride home.

Chapter Eight

Henry carried my two little bags inside the house. On the coffee table was a note from Isabelle, saying that she wouldn't be at church in the morning because she had to head back to school in the morning and that she would call us later. Henry and I sat down in the living room across from each other. I was on the love seat, and he sat down on the recliner.

I loved how wonderfully decorated the living room was, with the colors sage green and brown. The couches were a tan color with beautiful green and brown trimming. I noticed that color scheme had to be a woman's touch. *What woman though?* I asked myself. I came to the conclusion that perhaps it was Isabelle who picked out the colors.

While sitting the living room with him, I was a little nervous to be in the house alone with him, because I was feeling tempted to sleep next to him tonight. We chatted a little bit, some small talk about the weather and how the gas prices are still rising. I knew that he sensed some awkwardness too, but I was hoping it was because he was thinking about the same thing I was.

I watched his lips closely as he was talking to me. I imagined them on my body, kissing me gently. It's amazing how Henry never left me emotionally. He never married, and from what I know, he rarely dated. He practically waited for me to come back. It was as if he knew I would come back to him one day. *Maybe I should reward him with a little something, but I don't want to push myself on him.* I was so deep in my day dream that I had tuned him out without knowing it.

"I'm sorry, what were you saying?" I asked. I was a little embarrassed that he caught me daydreaming about him.

"I was asking you if you were going to church in the morning." I wondered to myself if he went to the same church that we used to go to years ago, the church where Isabelle was christened. I'm always up for church. I acknowledge God in everything that I do and everything that he has brought me through in my life. I was excited about going.

"Church sounds great. Are we going to Holy Cross?"

"Yeah, I still go there. Isabelle never liked that church. I think it's because my mother is always nagging her." *His mother, Miss Oda May.* I don't know how I should react to this, because I also have issues with his mother. Oda always judged me and she never liked me. I always believed it was because of my mother who she only knew as my alcoholic mother. Not only that, I'm sure she despised me for leaving Henry and Isabelle. I can't wait to see her reaction when she sees me for the first time in ten years.

She's one of the most hypocritical people that I know because Henry told me that she used to drink a lot when he was younger too, that is until she got saved, sanctified, and filled with the Holy Ghost. After Oda May stopped drinking she was officially better than the rest of the sinners in the world.

Oda May was mean-spirited back then and she was always envious of the way that Henry loved me. I will *have* to deal with her looking at me and whispering about me to the whole congregation telling people about how I abandoned my family and became an addict. Her version of the story would of course be filled with exaggeration. I took a deep breath and exhaled slowly. Breathing exercises to calm me down will definitely come in handy tomorrow.

"So your parents still go to Holy Cross, huh?" I was trying very hard to sound casual.

"Yeah and my father is one of the deacons now too," Henry replied.

I don't remember too much about his father; in fact, I forgot that he was alive. I know that his name was also Henry, his family and friends called him "Senior" for a nick name. He was rarely around before I left. I do know that Henry is the spitting image of his father. The times that I did see his father he spoke very little. He was a man who didn't talk unless he absolutely had something to say.

Henry caught the expression and walked over to me and rubbed my shoulders as if he was taking the worry away from me. I was so tempted to kiss him, but I was holding myself back. I loved him for being able to know what to do or say to make me feel better.

"I know what you're thinking," he said, massaging my shoulders gently.

"What am I thinking, Henry?" I asked softly.

"You're thinking about how you're going to deal with my mother tomorrow, aren't you?"

I nodded my head and tried to hold back my tears. I couldn't believe that I wanted to cry. I think I was scared of what his mother may say. Yup, she is just that mean; she could make a grown man cry.

"I know you're still afraid to face people. But the past is the past, okay? My mother is only human. She is not God, and therefore she can't judge you or condemn you." His words warmed my heart, and my only response was to turn around and kiss him.

I didn't realize I was kissing him until I felt the warmth of his hand on my face. I wanted more. I kissed him deeper and deeper. I wanted more of him; my body yearned for more. I wanted him to touch me and to explore me, to truly feel me and make love to me as if it were his last time to be with me. I loved this man, my husband. So many years we were apart and yet he waited for me. Henry waited for me to get rid of my demons so that I could be the woman and mother he knew I could be.

We helped each other up without separating. His tongue moved strategically in my mouth as our tongues tangoed and our moans harmonized like a love song. I never thought I could want to make love this bad. His arms felt very strong, and I felt very secure. More secure than I have ever felt in my whole life. There was no other man in the world for me.

We continued to hold each other close, and I could feel his yearning for me as we groaned and grinded with each other. *He has been saving himself for me all these years,* I thought to myself. I began to unbuckle his belt buckle. It was complicated at first, but I finally got to it. We simultaneously started to help each other undress as we found our way to the floor.

There was no way we going to bother to go upstairs. Right there on the Persian rug, we made love, and it was ecstatic. My body was electrified with his gentle motions and tender kisses. We completely wrapped ourselves in our love that night, and we did not go to sleep until we saw the sun. We were able to make up for lost time in a matter of hours. Before we dozed off, I wondered if we would wake in time for worship service.

Chapter Eight

Henry and I arrived at church thirty minutes late, but we made it in time for the sermon. We carefully took a seat in the back so we wouldn't disturb anyone. My body was still a little sore. I felt like I just ran a marathon or something, because the insides of my thighs were aching. Henry seemed a little tired, but we were very motivated to get up and go to church after a long night of lovemaking. This was my first time going to church in a while, and I have to be honest and admit that my mind wasn't really on what the preacher was saying. I didn't recognize him; he was a young man in his early thirties. He was walking back and forth and wiping sweat off his forehead, and the pianist was banging a key here and there when the preacher said something exciting.

After a while, I was getting a little uncomfortable because the wooden pews were hurting my back, and I was getting a headache because I didn't get to eat this morning. Henry noticed I was fidgeting and asked me if I was okay. I nodded and tried my hardest to pay attention to the preacher. When I was finally able to pay attention a little better, he was talking about walking in faith and about how faith is a process. I began to like his sermon; I even clapped a few times and said a few amens. I could feel Henry's hand behind my head. I would catch him nodding his head and saying: "All right now!" There's nothing like a man who loves church.

After the service was finally over, we waited in the back to catch his mother passing by. When Henry spotted her, we walked over to her. Oda May still looked the same. She was a tiny woman who wore bright red lipstick, dress suits with the biggest hats on Sunday. Today she wore a

three-piece lavender suit with matching hat. She reminded me of an Easter bouquet.

Oda May smiled at Henry and gave him a hug and a kiss on the cheek. I saw that his father was right behind her. He also hugged Henry, and then he spotted me. Henry Senior walked toward me, and I stood still. I didn't know if I should smile or not. I just gave him a little wave and grinned a little bit. He still looked the same; except he was a little bald at the top and had gray hair.

"Well, well, well, look here, Oda. Henry didn't tell us you were back," Senior said grinning.

Oda May appeared quickly next to her husband. She didn't smile or anything; her face was emotionless and that may have been a good sign.

"What in the world?" Oda May looked as if she was staring at a ghost. "When did you get back 'round here, girl?" she asked me, harshly. "Don't matter no way, you ain't staying is you?" *Wow.* I had forgotten how bad Oda May's English was. She is from the deep woods of Mississippi, but you'd think a person with English as bad as hers would have less to say about people.

"Oda, behave yourself. Why don't you greet the girl and be polite for once?" Senior spoke angrily to his wife.

"Don't matter why she here. She ain't nobody. Call yo'self a woman? Who you is just poppin' up like you got good sense? You ain't got good sense!" Oda May was sneering at me so much that she managed to get a little bit of red lip stick on her teeth.

"Mama, please. No one wants to hear all that!" Henry came to my rescue. I didn't even get one word out. I was relieved and irritated at the same time. *Who does she think she is anyway?* As soon as Oda May started going off, Senior crept out of the front of the church. He wanted nothing to do with his wife's loud ignorance. I had to say something to her, anything; I didn't want her to think I was a mute.

"It's nice to see your in good health, Miss Oda May," I said as sweetly as possible. I refused to let her get under my skin.

"I'm sure it is. How long you here for, girl?" She sneered so much that her eyes looked closed.

I was looking at Henry for a little help, but I decided to handle this one on my own. She was not about to get the best of me. "Well, I- I am actually here permanently," I answered proudly.

"Oh, really?" Oda May looked at her son and was silent for a moment. She appeared to be waiting for an explanation from him.

"Do she know, Henry? She don't know, do she?" Oda May said. *What didn't I know?* I asked myself. I looked to Henry for an answer, but he was still talking to his mother, trying to calm her down.

"Just as long as you know, Henry!" Oda May shouted to her son. "I raised you right. You know better! Now move!" Oda May walked away from her son and came over to me. She was so close, I could still see the bright red lipstick on her teeth, and her breath smelled like coffee and mints. She spoke softly but sternly as she said: "I feel sorry for the likes of you, girly, I really do. You jus' as clueless as a bad mystery story." *What did she say? A clueless mystery story? Who says stuff like that?* If I didn't know any better, I would have cussed that ignorant woman out from A to Z. *Who does she really think she is?*

The whole scene at church was playing in my mind for the rest of the day. I questioned Henry about it, and he nonchalantly brushed it off as his mother just wanting to make a scene at church because I was there. It was hard sleeping next to Henry that night because I was worried that he was hiding something from me. He assured me that there was nothing he was hiding from me.

I finally convinced myself that perhaps everything was going so perfectly between us that I was probably expecting something to go wrong. I made up in my mind that I wasn't going to look for something to go wrong anymore. I was going to count my blessings and be thankful for where God has brought me from and allowing me to get my family back.

Isabelle called late Sunday to check on us. We all spoke on speaker phone and enjoyed our long conversation about her plans for the next semester of school. I was so proud of Isabelle because she was doing so well in school and she had a head on her shoulders. I looked forward to us growing closer together over the years to come. My dream of being close to my only child was coming true and I wouldn't trade our relationship for anything in the world. I made a vow to love her the way a mother should love her daughter and be there for her always. *Thank you Lord for bringing me back to my family and for watching over us.*

Chapter Nine

Henry bought me a brand-new beige Honda Accord! It was definitely an unexpected gift. He surprised me by having it parked outside the house with a huge red ribbon on top of it. Henry gave me his credit card to go shopping for new clothes, since I will be starting my new job he got me at the Veteran Memorial hospital. He wanted me to be able to be independent while he was away at work and not have not to catch a bus or call a taxi.

I was also excited about my job because I hadn't had a real job in a few years and Henry was able to pull some strings for me with a "friend in charge" for a receptionist position. I was more than ready to get in my car and go on my shopping spree. I couldn't wait to buy some new clothes that I was in need of.

I was surprised that I still knew my way around the city. I'm used to traveling on a bus, and it's different when you're driving because the streets look different. I decided that I would park my vehicle in an underground car garage and walk downtown to shop in the stores there. As I was walking downtown, I was glad that I dressed for the weather and wore a sweat suit, because it was—as I call it—"Chicago windy" outside. However, it was still a beautiful day to spend my loving husband's money.

I walked into five stores and was able to find two pairs of dress shoes and four outfits that I absolutely loved. I made sure that I got Henry a shirt and tie and Isabelle a sundress. It felt good to go shopping like I did back in the old days. The last thing I wanted to do today was get a makeover. I was certainly in need of a new look to go with my new outfits. It felt like I was on cloud nine and I didn't want to get off either. I haven't felt this

good in years. I finally got my rightful place back where I belonged and life was good. God is good and I know His mercy endures forever. *Thank you Jesus!* He certainly has seen me through a lot of obstacles in my life. When I decided to turn my life over to Him, things just lined up for me the way He saw fit. I never thought in a million years that I would be where I am today. God is definitely in control of everything.

    I locked the bags in the trunk of my car and walked across the street where I saw a salon. I was greeted right away when I walked in and led to an open chair. I looked at the old me one last time. *Bye Darla!* I said to myself smiling from ear to ear. I wanted to have a new look to go with my new life. I cut all my hair off in the back and left enough at the top for the stylist to do a swooped bang that I always liked. The makeup lady taught me how to apply makeup that would make me look like I wasn't wearing any. She even showed me how blend colors for my eye makeup and how to choose my lip and foundation colors. I loved my new look and I felt better than I had in a decade. Now I couldn't wait to get home to my hubby and show him my new look.

Chapter Ten

As I was walking out of the salon and heading back to the car, I spotted the woman I saw at the park a few weeks ago. I didn't recognize her right away because she looked like a pleasant human being; that is, until she saw me. When she recognized me, her face automatically went into that familiar scowl and then she began walking towards me. Up close, she was actually very pretty; too bad she's always frowning up her face though. She was dressed in a beige suit and heels with her hair cropped in a neatly cut bob. She stopped in front of me and looked me up and down.

"So I see you got yourself all fixed up." *What is her problem?* All I could think to myself is that I didn't want to go to jail today.

"Yes, I just got my hair cut at the salon," I decided to still be polite to her. I refused to let her get me upset and sweat out my hairstyle or my makeup.

"I remember you from the park. You were with my man, Henry." *Excuse me? Your man Henry?* I felt bad for her because she was truly delusional.

"Sweetheart, what do you mean by that? What makes you think he is your man?" I asked. I felt my anger rising up in my throat. I didn't want to throw her into the street and let a bus run her over because that would be murder in the second degree, right? I had to collect myself and figure why this poor thing was tripping.

"Why do you think Henry is your man? Are you really that delusional?" I asked her casually. I didn't want her to think that she was getting to me.

"No, honey, *you* are. We were actually engaged." She held out her hand and showed me a small diamond ring. *What—engaged? How? What?*

"Engaged?" I asked. I was truly bewildered at she just told me.

"Yes, engaged. He called it off when *you* showed up on his doorstep. I have been waiting for him to marry me for almost three years now, and when we finally set a date for the wedding, you decided that you finally wanted to come back. He was ready to move on and finalize the divorce papers until you came and tore our family apart." *Family? Engaged?* I could not understand what was going on right now.

"You decided that you didn't want to be a mother or a wife anymore. My son needs his father in his life—"

"Your *son*?" I asked. I wanted to scream at the top of my lungs. *Was I being played this whole time? Was Henry trying to get back at me for hurting him?*

"Henry the third actually. He wanted to keep the family name going." *What? His son? Henry has another child?* I suddenly felt the stabs of betrayal in the pit of my stomach and my heart. *This was all a set up to get back at me.*

"I had no idea about this," I said sadly shaking my head. Tears were welling up in my eyes. I refused to let them fall. *Whatever you do, don't cry in front of this woman! Suck it up! Fast!*

"I know you didn't. I'm just angry that he couldn't even face me at the park that day. He completely ignored me, knowing what he did to me." The woman flipped her hair out of her eyes and smirked at me. She was certainly getting pleasure from seeing me hurt. One tear finally fell and I was suddenly feeling really silly. *How could I have even believed that Henry wasn't with anyone else all these years? I feel so stupid.*

"How did you know that he would even be at the park?" I asked, curiously.

"I used to work for Henry as his secretary. I practically made up the company calendar. I know the dates, times, and places of all the company functions by heart." It didn't take much for me to notice that she was obviously very much into her job. "When I got pregnant," she continued brushing the hair out of her eyes, "we thought it was best that I didn't work for him anymore." She politely waited patiently for the next phase of the conversation.

"How old is your son now?" I really didn't want to know, but I needed facts if I was going to confront Henry about his little mistress. I really

wanted to know as much detail as possible because I intended to get a full explanation of everything from Henry later on.

"He will be five this year. Look, I'm sorry you had to find out from me. Henry should have been man enough to tell you." With that being said, she flipped her hair and walked off.

I didn't even catch her name. Clearly, Henry had left her for me. Clearly, he loved her some kind of way to want to have a child with her, marry her, and divorce me. *I just can't even think straight. How can this be happening after all these weeks of total bliss?*

I was able to make it to the car without passing out. I wanted to shout, scream, kick, and run. Instead, I put my head on the steering wheel and sobbed until the mascara and eyeliner burned the corneas of eyes.

Chapter Eleven

I couldn't wait for Henry to get home. I was in the kitchen, pacing back and forth angrily. *Who does he think he is?* I was ready to pack my things and leave, but I decided to face him first. The phone was irritating me, ringing off the hook, and I was *way* too angry to answer it. I think I was more hurt than anything else. *How could this be happening? Was I being punished or something? Is this what karma feels like?*

Now I began to understand things a little better. My woman instincts kicked in, and I started to remember the incident at church with Henry and his mother, it began to make sense what they were whispering about. Oda May *had* to have known about this. But I remember plainly when Isabelle told me that her father hardly dated. *She would have mentioned an engagement wouldn't she have? Did Isabelle lie to me? Did she know about her brother?*

I walked into the living room and looked around. *A woman's touch. Yeah, her touch.* He even had her decorating up in here. *In my house? Oh, hell no! When did Henry turn into a conniving little liar? We made love on that rug, the one she probably picked out!* Hate and fury rose up in my throat. I went back into the kitchen and started pacing again. *How can I be angry at him after what I did? I should forgive him. But how could he do this to me?* I asked myself, sadly.

Why did this have to happen right now? Why not a few years from now? Why today? Why this moment after everything has been going so well? This is too much to bear. God, this is too much to bear. Who am I not to forgive, though? I have been forgiven, right? I could just walk away and forget I was even here. I should just leave and let him go be with her. He was about to

marry her, and I don't want to ruin his plans. I'm just gonna pack my things and head back to the boarding house. I don't need this pressure in my life, not right now. I don't need this. I came back hoping something good could finally happen to me, but now I know it can't; there is no way.

On my way back up the stairs, I heard the front door open. *Oh, this Negro 'bout to get it!* I was pumped up, ready to rumble, and ready to give him a peace of my mind! I quickly started back down the stairs and saw Isabelle standing at the bottom of the stairs.

"Hey!" she exclaimed. I met her down the stairs and gave her a hug. I didn't want her to know that I as angry right away. I surprised myself at how quickly I calmed down.

"Hey, sweetie, your back from school already?" I asked, trying to sound calm.

"I have a week break until the next class starts. What's wrong?" Isabelle is just like her father; she can pick up other people's emotions. I didn't know exactly what to tell her. I just sat her down on the couch and decided to just level with her.

"I just found out some information about your father, and it's bothering me a little bit." I felt my heart beating really fast. I wanted to ask her flat out why she lied to me, but the words didn't come out.

"What kind of information?" Isabelle asked, curiously.

"This woman approached me today when I was downtown shopping and she told me that she was engaged to Henry and that they had a son together." I looked at Isabelle and waited for her reaction.

"Oh, please don't tell me you ran into Keisha Manning." Isabelle shook her head and laughed. She caught me off guard with her laughing. *I figured she would get a hoot out of making a fool out of me.* "That woman is a lunatic. I told Dad not to go out with her. She's crazy."

What just happened here? I was so confused right now.

"Wh- what do you mean?" I was totally baffled by this information. I was feeling a mixture of emotions from relief to stupidity.

"See, Keisha was Daddy's secretary, and his friend set her up with him so that he could have someone go to the annual company dinner with. To make a long story short, she began to obsess over him and wanted to be with him. When Daddy turned her down, she screamed sexual harassment falsely and got fired. He was going to sue her, but he felt bad for her and changed his mind. He even offered to pay for a psychiatric evaluation and rehab but she refused."

I couldn't believe what I was hearing. This whole time, I had been angry for nothing, over a *crazy* girl. I still wasn't convinced, though.

"What about the little boy she told me about? She said it was Henry's. She said she even named him Henry the third."

Isabelle burst out laughing. *I wish she would stop laughing.* I was becoming irritated because this situation wasn't funny at all to me, this was a very serious matter!

"I'm sorry; I don't mean to laugh at you. It's just that Keisha will *not* give up. She just wanted to upset you that's all. I hope you didn't let her get to you." Isabelle gave me a hug and was obviously trying not to chuckle.

"Yeah well she sounded pretty convincing to me, especially when she was talking about her son." I was beginning to feel a little better, but I still wanted to hear Henry's explanation in his own words.

"If it will make you feel better, I don't even think *she* knows who the father is. I know it's not Daddy's, because that little boy looks nothing like him for one thing. I bet she told you that she was engaged and that Daddy broke off the wedding right? I bet she said that." Isabelle nodded her head, she was so sure that she was right.

"How did you know that?" I couldn't help but laugh out loud this time. This whole situation was so crazy.

"Keisha saw me walking in the mall with Dad and followed me into the nail salon. She sat down next to me and was telling me that Dad was cheating on her with me and that she was calling the wedding off because she was tired of him cheating on her. The whole time, Keisha didn't even know that I was his *daughter*. I guess it's because I look a little older than most girls my age." I knew I got upset because I was afraid of loosing my family again, now I was ecstatic that loosing my family was not an issue anymore.

"Wow, I can't believe I was so upset earlier over a crazy girl," I admitted.

"Don't worry about it; it happens sometimes, I guess. Don't worry about her. She is perfectly harmless," Isabelle reassured.

"But she looks so *normal*," I said, laughing.

"Don't worry, Mom, most crazy people do." Isabelle kissed me on the cheek and bounced upstairs. I don't think she realized she called me "Mom." That's the best thing I heard all decade. *Mom.* The sound of that name rang in my ears like music.

My heart felt a little lighter until I remembered Oda May and Henry's conversation on Sunday. *I will ask him about it tonight,* I reminded myself.

Everything seemed to be back to normal except for that one little detail. I still have no clue what Oda May was talking about and I wanted to know! I couldn't wait to see Henry tonight and tell him that I love him. As long there is no bad news or secrets; I planned to make sure that everything was all cleared up so that we could finally move on with our lives.

Chapter Twelve

When Henry got home that night, I put a note on the door telling him to meet me in the guest room. I waited patiently for him on the bed in the lingerie that I bought from a boutique downtown. I decided not to bring up the incident that happened today. I'm grateful that I found out the truth before I decided to do something drastic. I couldn't wait for Henry to rip off this little black number that covered the right places and showed off the wrong places, if you know what I mean.

Henry came through the door; I could see the delighted expression on his face. When he saw what I was wearing, he smiled and loosened his tie and came right over to me. He got undressed down to his T-shirt and boxers and got in the bed with me.

"Wow, you look sensational. Is *this* how you're spending my money now? I'm glad you start working soon," he chuckled. I leaned over him and planted a gentle kiss on his cheek.

"I really missed you today," I said softly.

"Me too, baby, me too. I have something for you." *A surprise! I love surprises!* Henry reached into his pocket and pulled out a little white box. To my great surprise, he got off the bed and got down on one knee and opened the box. My heart was beating so fast, I couldn't believe it. *Was he proposing?* Henry opened the box, and in it was a little gold ring with a diamond in it.

"Darla, since you been back, I finally understand truly what love is." I couldn't believe what Henry was doing. I felt so special. He reached for my hand and continued his speech. "Love is about forgiveness and kindness. I love you genuinely, and I would do anything in the world for

you. I want us to renew our vows and start over for good this time. What do you think?"

I couldn't fight the tears, and all I could do was nod my head, because I had the biggest knot in my throat. Henry put the ring on my finger, and I realized that everything I have been through in my life has led up to this point where we are today. I hugged him tightly, and then I looked him in his eyes.

"Henry, I have two questions for you," I said to him softly. I was trying very hard not to ruin the moment.

"What is it, baby?" Henry asked me attentively.

"This may sound crazy right now, but that day you and your mother were fussing in church, what were you guys arguing about?" I don't know the answer that I was looking for, but I just wanted him to be honest with me.

"Well since you want to know so *badly*, my mother wanted me to tell you that she doesn't like you and she wished that you would disappear." We burst out laughing so hard that we both fell backwards. "I told her that if she didn't like you so bad she should go tell you herself!" *As if that was a surprise! His mother doesn't like anyone.*

"What's your second question?" Henry asked me tenderly.

"Who decorated the living room and the bedrooms?" The question suddenly sounded silly. Henry thought it was a joke, but when he saw my facial expression, he knew I was dead serious.

"I hired an interior decorator. Why? You don't like what she did? Do you wanna change it?" *A decorator! Phew! Okay, now I can move on with my life.*

"No, never mind, honey, let's just enjoy the night, okay?" I kissed him and pulled him up on the bed.

"Baby, why are we in the guest room?" Henry asked.

"Because I don't want to wake up Isabelle; she's in her room," I whispered throwing the covers over our head. We chuckled like little kids playing hide-and-seek.

"Henry?"

"Yeah?"

"Let's never go to sleep angry with each other or lie to each other okay?" I suggested softly.

"Never that, baby, never that. Now let's stop talking." Henry tickled me under the covers and we played all night long. The gift of love and

forgiveness are the greatest gifts I have ever experienced. Love truly does conquer all.

I couldn't be happier than I was today, and I knew from that point on, I would be happy like this forever. Hey, why not? Everyone deserves love and happiness in their lives.

Proverbs Woman

When a man finds a wife, he finds a good thing.
What's a woman to do when she loves her husband more than "life" itself?

Chapter One

Lauren Morgan admired, honored, and loved her husband dearly. He was the best thing that ever happened to her. She woke up before him in the morning just to look at him as he slept. Lauren would gently stroke his cheek and whisper into his ear that she loved him. She would then get up to pick out his work clothes, iron them to a crisp, and then shine his shoes.

Afterward, she would run down to the kitchen to fix him breakfast. Breakfast was the same every morning, just the way her husband Mike liked it: three scrambled eggs with cheese, three slices of bacon, two pancakes, decaffeinated coffee, and an apple for the road. Lauren was never tired of pleasing her man. While other women were complaining about their men being pushy and needy, Lauren loved the fact that her husband needed her.

After the morning routine, Lauren would quickly get dressed. She didn't have a job to get ready for in the morning; she just wanted Mike to always see her looking her best. Lauren conveniently had her wardrobe planned the night before so that it wouldn't take her long to get ready before Mike woke up.

Today she was going to wear her favorite pale yellow Ralph Lauren sundress with the matching Jimmy Chu shoes. She quickly slipped on the dress and tried her best not to wake Mike. Lauren unwrapped her hair and brushed it down to perfection. Mike loved the fact that Lauren was a black woman with long hair and preferred that she wear it down to show off her long mane that was all hers.

Lauren chuckled, remembering the night that they met at a mutual friend's party. *Mike was so fine,* Lauren thought, *and he still is too.* The first time she laid her eyes on Mike, Lauren knew that he was out of her league. He reminded her of the guys on the S-curl boxes. He was dark with gorgeous skin, his hair was always cut neatly, and his beard was trimmed so neatly and carefully. The night they met, Lauren tried hard not to admire his body, how tall he was, and the fact that she could see the muscles through his polo shirt.

She didn't bother to approach him that night, because she figured there was no way he could ever be into her. Then, Lauren saw him walking toward her as if he was in slow motion. When he got to her, he began to touch and stroke her hair that fell past her shoulders. She was too stunned by how fine he was to stop and ask him if he was crazy.

"You don't see too many black girls with long hair. Is it yours?" Mike asked the first time they met.

Lauren was shocked by his question but glad that she could say: "Yes, it's mine." She always thought her hair was her best asset. That is until Mike helped her to see herself as an attractive and sexy woman. Lauren started to wear makeup over her small, light brown eyes, and lip gloss over her round lips. It wasn't much, but it was a start. Lauren even began wearing designer clothes, to make her look more sophisticated.

One day, Mike told her that she could have been a supermodel because she always dressed like she was in a magazine or in a fashion show. Her growing confidence in herself made her feel sexier as they were dating. Lauren no longer saw herself as the light-skinned girl with long hair. She saw herself as a tall, sexy, intelligent black woman.

Five years into the marriage, Lauren was sure that she had found her soul mate, a man who gave her everything and someone who loved her more than she could ever love herself. Lauren made up her mind that she was the luckiest woman in the world.

When Mike came down for breakfast, Lauren was at the table, reading the newspaper. As soon as he came into the kitchen, she quickly got up and fixed his plate. Lauren didn't throw the food on the plate the way most women would. Instead, she strategically put the eggs on the right side of the plate. The bacon was always placed on the other side of the plate so that they didn't touch the eggs. The pancakes were served on a separate plate with a small pitcher of syrup, and the coffee was poured into his favorite morning mug.

Lauren never took the apple out of the refrigerator until it was time for him to go out the door, because she knew that Mike liked his apple to be cold so that it would make the crispy crunchy sound when he bit into it. Sure, he was picky and meticulous, but she didn't mind making her man happy, by all means necessary.

Mike sat down at the table and beckoned Lauren to the table. She caught his gesture and went over to him quickly.

"Did you pick up the dry cleaning yesterday?" Mike asked.

"No, baby, it wasn't ready yet. I can get it today," Lauren said, bending down and giving him a kiss on the forehead.

"Yeah, do that for me," he replied. Lauren sighed and ignored the harshness she heard in his voice. She was determined to have a good breakfast with him before they went their separate ways for the day.

Lauren placed the food on the table in front of her husband. Again, she did it strategically, the way he liked it. The plate of eggs and bacon was to his right and the pancakes with the pitcher of syrup were placed to the left. She put the coffee diagonally across from the plate with the bacon and eggs on it so that he wouldn't have to reach over the food to get it. Mike smelled the food before he started to eat. He wanted to make sure that he couldn't smell the cheese too much. Mike liked the taste of cheese, but he didn't like to smell it on his eggs.

Lauren knew when Mike was satisfied with his food because he would start eating and pouring his syrup. She made herself a bowl of cereal and sat across from him. He didn't like her to eat heavy foods, because he wanted her to keep her small frame and not put on any weight. That's why Mike didn't want Lauren to get pregnant, because he didn't want her to "loose her shape." Lauren wanted children badly, but he always made sure that she took her

birth control pills faithfully. She was always hoping that he would change his mind one day.

Mike looked up from his food, and Lauren caught his gaze at her. He pointed to his cup for more coffee, and she quickly went and got it.

"What are your plans for today?" *Aw, he is always so concerned about me*, Lauren thought. She loved that Mike wanted to know where she would be and what she would be doing. That made her feel like he cared about her safety.

"I'm supposed to meet Rose and Dawn at the restaurant today for lunch," Lauren replied.

"I don't like those women; they talk too much," Mike said stiffly.

"You don't want me to go?" Lauren asked. She was willing to change her plans, because she respected her husbands' feelings.

"No, you can go; the dry cleaners are right across the street. You can head over there after your little gossip session with the ladies." With that said, he pushed his chair back and got up from the table. He grabbed his briefcase and Lauren handed him his apple. Mike told Lauren to have dinner hot when he gets back and then he was out of the door.

Lauren sat down and finished her bowl of cereal even though it was a little soft. The house was silent, and she felt lonely. The house was very big, and no one was in it but her. She went up to the bedroom, made the bed, and cleaned up the bathroom. Cleaning up for Mike was a tedious job; he never hired a maid because he didn't think they could do as good a job as Lauren. She was flattered by that, so she always made sure that everything was done in the house above and beyond his standards.

Lauren went through all five rooms and two and a half bathrooms to make sure that everything was clean and orderly. Lauren always wondered why they got such a big house if they weren't going to have children. *Maybe one day he will finally change his mind and want to have children with me to fill up these rooms,* Lauren thought to herself sadly.

Chapter Two

By the time she cleaned the whole house, it was time to meet her friends at the Italian restaurant downtown. She wasn't thrilled about meeting them for lunch, simply because they did gossip and sometimes her friends could be a little conceited. Rose was a divorced fifty-year-old woman who was bitter, but at the same time she was happy, because alimony kept her champagne lifestyle afloat. Dawn was younger than Rose and in a marriage where she knew her husband was cheating, but she decided to stay in the marriage for financial security. Lauren was happy that her marriage was nothing like theirs. She was proud that her husband came home every night, even if it was about two or three o'clock in the morning at times. At least she could say that for five years, she never slept alone.

Lauren walked into the restaurant and saw Rose sitting at the table by the window. She smiled at Lauren and stood up to hug her. Lauren noticed that she looked like she lost a little more weight since the last time she saw her. Rose went from a size eight to a size fourteen almost immediately after she found out that her husband was cheating on her. She practically ate herself to death from depression and anger. *She is finally losing weight now,* Lauren said to herself. She noticed that Rose's dark skin was glowing with happiness. Lauren wondered to herself if her happiness was a reflection of a new love in her life.

Just as Lauren sat down, Dawn came to the table and cheerfully said hello to the other two women. Dawn never told her age, but Lauren figured her to be around her age, in her mid-thirties. Lauren always liked Dawn because she was more down-to-earth and she didn't want to gossip as much as Rose did. Lauren always admired how beautiful and honest Dawn was.

Dawn was the shortest of the three women; she stood about five feet two and always wore her hair cut short. Rose and Dawn sat next to each other while Lauren sat on the other side with an empty chair next to hers.

"So, how is everything going, ladies?" Rose said. She spoke behind her menu and then looked up to see who would answer first.

"Well, everything has been all right. I can't complain," said Dawn. She always tried to respectfully leave her personal life out of conversation. Dawn didn't mind listening, but she never really shared.

"What about you, Miss Lauren, how are things at home?" Dawn asked. Lauren was surprised that she asked her question that way. It was usually Rose who wanted to know how everything was at someone else's home. Lauren nodded and shrugged her shoulders, trying to be nonchalant about her answer.

"Same here, can't complain." Lauren was satisfied with her answer; she quickly tried to look occupied by looking at the menu.

"So what are you having to eat, Lauren?" Rose asked, putting down her menu. Dawn called for the waitress to come over.

"I think I will just have a salad," Lauren answered.

Dawn put her menu down and looked at Lauren with her eye brows raised. "A salad?" Dawn asked confused.

"You not hungry?" Rose asked. Lauren noticed that Rose had some red lipstick stuck on her front tooth.

Lauren hesitated with her answer. She didn't want to sound silly to them.

"I want to watch my figure, that's all," Lauren said shrugging her shoulders. Just then, the waitress appeared and she was relieved that all the attention was off of her for a moment.

The waitress started with Rose who ordered veggie lasagna, and Dawn ordered the same. They both looked at Lauren to see if she would change her order, but Lauren still ordered the salad. The waitress grabbed the menus and disappeared.

"You must have eaten already or something," Rose said curiously.

"No, I just want to watch what I eat. Mike wants me to keep my figure." *Uh oh,* Lauren thought to herself. She may have said too much. Lauren knew that Rose was going to dig deeper to get her to say something juicy, while Dawn sat back and looked off into the distance, wanting no part of the conversation for now.

"Why are you worried about what he thinks about you? You need to do for yourself, eat what you want to eat. You won't die, will you?"

Lauren felt irritation sinking in. She was ready for the lunch meeting to be over with. *Mike was right,* she thought angrily, *I should not have come.* Lauren was grateful when Dawn changed the subject.

"So how come you weren't at the Country Club Ball last month?" she asked.

"Oh, I didn't know about it. When was it?" Lauren asked, grateful for the change of conversation.

Rose took it upon herself to rub it in that only the most exclusive club members get an invitation. She and Dawn got one, and so did a few of her neighbors. Lauren didn't remember seeing an invitation, but she was sure that if there was one, Mike must have thrown it away, because he hated formal parties.

"Oh, Mike and I don't really go to those kinds of functions, so it would not have mattered if we got one or not." Lauren saw Rose nudge Dawn on the arm.

Rose smiled at Lauren from across the table.

"Well, me *and* Dawn have something to tell you," Rose said, casually.

"What? What are you guys keeping from me?" Lauren asked curiously, looking back and forth from one person to the next. The waitress came over to the table with the food. Lauren's appetite was suddenly gone; she was ready to go because she was feeling a little stuffy and uncomfortable. Dawn was digging into her food, but Rose had not touched her plate yet.

"Well, that's funny that you didn't go to the party," Rose said, trying to sound mysterious. Dawn nudged Rose in the arm and shook her head. Lauren was growing impatient.

"Oh, why is that?" she asked.

Lauren could tell that Rose was trying to be careful with the next words she was going to say. She stole a quick glance at Dawn and saw that her head was down as if she refused to be a part of the conversation.

"Well," Rose started off slowly, "I saw Mike at the dance, but I didn't see you there." She finally cut into her lasagna, chewed, and swallowed. Lauren could have sworn that she was trying to savor what she had to say for a delicate moment. Lauren immediately made up her mind that she was ready to go. *What's the point of staying?* She thought to herself, impatiently.

"Well, I didn't know about the party, I told you that just now," Lauren said defensively as she tried to compose herself and not let her temper get the best of her.

"That's funny that you didn't know. I found it strange that you weren't there and even more when I saw him there with someone else."

Lauren's stomach suddenly felt full, but she never had a bite of her salad. *Another woman? Yeah, right, not Mike.* Lauren convinced herself that Rose didn't know what she was talking about. Dawn still hadn't said a word.

"Tell her, Dawn, that you saw him there too with that other woman." Rose nudged Dawn, but she shook her head and refused to be a scapegoat for the gossip that was taking place. Dawn was getting upset. She put her fork down and wiped her mouth with the napkin. She turned to Rose and looked her straight in the eyes.

"Why is it any of your business what she has going on in *her* marriage? Why don't you just let it go and mind your own business?" Dawn surprised Lauren with how loud her voice was getting. "Did it ever occur to you that just because you saw her husband talking to the hostess at the ball, don't mean that he is *sleeping* with her. Get a life Rose." Dawn quickly took a deep breath and continued with her meal. She caught Laurens' bewildered gaze and winked at her.

Rose shrugged her shoulders and continued to eat as if nothing had happened. She looked at Lauren with a smirk on her face, trying to hold in her laughter. Lauren was so fed up with Rose that she quickly gathered her purse, keys, and sunglasses. She went into her wallet and put a twenty-dollar bill on the table. Lauren was too upset to say goodbye; she just walked out and went across the street to the dry cleaners with a lot on her mind.

Chapter Three

Lauren made it home just in time to make dinner. She decided that she would make a simple meal of baked chicken with jasmine rice and mixed vegetables. The house was cold and dark, but she didn't mind because she was used to it. After Lauren cooked dinner, she set the table and then sat down on the couch. She hadn't eaten since breakfast, and she wasn't feeling like herself. Her head was spinning and her chest felt like it was on fire. Lauren glanced at the clock and decided that she had a few hours to lie down and take a nap before Mike got home.

Lauren woke up and realized that she may have overslept. She jumped up off the couch and looked at her watch. It was eight thirty. Mike should have been home an hour ago. *He must be leaving the office late,* she thought. She dialed his number from her cell phone and didn't get an answer, so she decided to eat without him. By the time she finished eating, it was nine fifteen and Mike still had not called to say he would be late. Lauren felt herself getting angry and sick at the same time. She must have eaten too fast, because she suddenly felt nauseated.

What is wrong with me today? She asked herself. It wasn't like her to leave the kitchen messy with dishes in the sink and food on the stove. She slowly made her way upstairs; she was feeling very weak and light headed. Lauren thought a hot and steamy shower would make her feel better, but it only made her feel worse. She stretched herself on the bed in her robe and fell asleep once more.

Lauren woke up to someone tapping her heavily on the shoulder. She slowly opened her eyes and saw Mike standing over her with his hands on his hips.

"Lauren, what the hell is going on? Why is the kitchen, the bathroom, and the bedroom in a mess?" Mike was obviously upset, and Lauren didn't have the energy to try to explain herself. She put her head back on the pillow and placed her hands over her face.

Mike was still standing over her, yelling about how he was expecting to come home to a clean house and a warm dinner. Lauren caught a glimpse of the time on the digital radio. It was almost three o'clock in the morning. She climbed off the bed slowly and walked towards the bathroom.

Her husband continued to yell obscenities to her and tell her how worthless she was. Lauren turned to her husband to speak, but instead she collapsed to her knees and vomited.

Mike was livid when he saw Lauren throwing up on the white carpet. He quickly grabbed her bath towel off the bed to cover the vomit.

"Woman, what is wrong with you?" Mike asked angrily. Lauren reached up her hands for Mike to help her up, but instead he kicked the dirty towel over to her in disgust.

"Now I gotta get a new rug 'cause of your dumb ass," he sneered.

"I'm sorry Mike, I don't feel well," Lauren said weakly.

"Look, I'm sleeping in the other room; I don't feel like smelling that funky ass vomit in here. Make sure you clean that shit up," Mike said as he was gathering his night clothes. Lauren felt hurt and abandoned.

"Mike, I need you tonight. Why don't you lay down with me?" Lauren asked tearfully.

"You know how I feel about smells," Mike said as he walked out the door.

Lauren let the tears fall down her face. She didn't know what was going on with her body today. *Maybe the chicken was bad,* she thought, sadly.

Lauren mustered up all the energy she had and cleaned up the vomit. She took another shower and decided to go meet Mike in the other room. When she got there, he was already asleep on his side. She climbed into the bed and put her arms around him. Mike shifted his position and turned away from her to lie on his stomach.

"Go back to the room," he demanded.

"I took another shower," Lauren explained. "I feel a little better. Must have been something that I ate." She was hoping that Mike would let her stay with him. *Perhaps we can make love tonight,* she thought hopefully.

"Baby, I'm gonna go to the doctor office tomorrow and get checked out. I think I have a stomach virus or something," Lauren said. She realized that Mike had fallen back asleep because he was snoring lightly. She began

to rub his back softly hoping that he would shift positions again and hold her.

Lauren was convinced that although Mike had a hard exterior, he loved her deeply; it was just hard for him to show it sometimes.

Chapter Four

When Lauren woke up, she saw that Mike was already gone. *Wow, I must have been really tired,* she thought to herself. She rolled over and looked at the clock on the wall. It was almost eleven o'clock. Lauren never slept that late. Mike was already at work; he didn't want to wake her, so he left quietly. *How considerate of him, she thought, smiling.*

As she threw back the covers, she remembered that she had to make an appointment with her doctor immediately, to find out what was wrong with her. She had never felt this way before. Her head was still hurting, and she still didn't have an appetite for anything but saltine crackers. Lauren dialed the number to her doctor's office and to her surprise, she was able to get an appointment within the hour. She quickly got dressed and headed out the door.

When Lauren arrived at the doctor's office, the smell of Pine Sol attacked her nose and immediately her eyes started to water. *What an unusual reaction,* she thought. Looking around at the people in the waiting room, she saw a lot of people with tissues who were coughing. *I must have what they have,* she said to herself.

"Are you here for an appointment or are you a walk-in?" A woman asked from behind the glass.

Lauren walked up to the window and spoke into the open slot. "Um yes, I have an appointment with Dr. Smith. She said I could be seen before lunch time."

The receptionist behind the glass began typing into the computer and looked up at Lauren. "Name, please?"

"Lauren Morgan." The woman nodded her head and gave her a paper to sign.

"You must have what everyone else in here has. There is a virus going around it seems like the whole town is in here."

Lauren nodded her head, "It's a good thing I called this morning before the crowd got here then."

Lauren signed the paper and the receptionist directed her to the room, where her doctor was waiting for her.

When Lauren walked into the examination room, she started to shake a little. *Am I nervous? Or am I cold?* She asked herself.

"Well, hello, Mrs. Morgan. How are you today?"

"I could be better, Dr. Smith. I may have that virus everyone keeps talking about." Lauren laughed a little bit to shake off the nervousness.

"Well, let me check you out and have a look. I have to draw some blood, and I need you to pee in this cup for me. I will run everything through the lab and then be right back. It won't take but a few minutes."

She handed Lauren the cup, and she went into the bathroom. Lauren didn't want to have any blood drawn; like most people, she hated needles.

Dr. Smith had a nurse already in the examination room, prepping the needle and the little containers the blood would go in. The nurse instructed Lauren to place the cup of urine on the counter and then invited her to have a seat on the chair.

The blood came out quickly when the nurse pierced her skin. Lauren felt like she was about to pass out at the sight of her own blood.

"What is the blood test for?" Lauren asked trying her best not to sound worried.

"Well, we run different tests to see what type of virus you may have, so that we know what kind of medicine we want to give you."

The nurse bandaged up her arm quickly. *It wasn't so bad,* Lauren thought. *It happened quicker than I thought. I should call Mike to tell him what's going on. He hasn't called me yet today to check on me.* As she dialed his number, she realized that she didn't have any service. Lauren sighed heavily and decided to look at magazines while she waited for her results.

Dr. Smith finally came back; it seemed like she took forever. She sat down on her swivel chair and looked through some papers on her clipboard.

"Come have a seat, Mrs. Morgan. I have some news for you." Dr. Smith patted the chair that was across from her. Lauren felt as if she was about to walk off the plank to her death.

"Well, what kind of virus do I have? Will I be sick long?" Lauren asked.

"The tests show that you don't have a virus. I had the lab run it twice just to be sure. They show something else." Lauren tried to study the doctor's face, as if that would help her to figure out what *exactly* was going on.

"How has your cycle been lately?" the doctor asked.

Lauren answered quickly, "My periods have been fine. I haven't missed one at all. Why?" Lauren was getting nervous. *Lord, please let everything be okay with me,* she prayed.

"Are you on birth control?" Dr. Smith asked curiously as she was taking down notes.

"Yes, I've been on it for a few years now. I don't understand; if I don't have the virus, what's wrong with me then?" Lauren was trying her best to remain calm. *What could be wrong with me?* She wondered fretfully.

The doctor sighed and put down her clipboard. Her face, unbelievably, had no expression on it. Lauren was becoming more scared.

"Well, I don't know how you are going to take this, but you're a little over three months pregnant."

Lauren's heart skipped a beat.

"What do you mean? How is that possible?" Tears began to pour out of her eyes. She didn't know why she was crying. Shouldn't she be happy? But then, how could she be? *Mike doesn't want kids,* she thought. *What am I going to do?* The tears continued pouring like a steady stream. She wasn't sure if they were happy tears or sad tears.

"I assume you weren't trying to get pregnant."

"He doesn't want kids," Lauren whispered.

"Do *you* want kids?" the doctor asked softly.

Lauren nodded her head yes slowly. "But not at the expense of my marriage. I respected the fact that he didn't want kids from the very beginning. I was okay with that when I married him. But now … I don't know … How could this happen?" Lauren began to sob uncontrollably.

"You have options, you know. You have to decide very soon if you want to keep the baby or not, because you're pretty far along. There are no local clinics here that will give you an abortion if you are already in your more

than halfway through your second trimester. So you have a lot to think about these next few days. Call me if you need anything."

Dr. Smith patted Lauren on the back as she left the room, and Lauren was by herself. She had so many questions and didn't know who to ask. Pregnant? Is it a boy or girl? Should she keep it? Save her marriage? Ruin her marriage? Lauren did feel a bit of hope; maybe Mike would be happy and change his mind about having a child after all.

There was a knock at the door and the nurse came in.

"Sorry to bother you; Dr. Smith wanted me to bring you a prescription for prenatal vitamins to be filled. She wanted to know if you had any other questions or concerns."

The nurse put the prescription down on the counter in front of Lauren.

"Uh, no, I don't have any questions, thank you."

Chapter Five

When Lauren got home, her mind continued to race back and forth. Should she tell Mike or not? What if he would be happy, then what? She still had four hours until Mike would be home. There was so much to do, she had to cook and clean, and do laundry. Her head started to hurt and her stomach felt like it had a million butterflies flying around in it.

Lauren went into the kitchen and fixed a sandwich. She had to force herself to eat. The baby ... what in the world was happening to her? *Do I want this baby?* She asked herself sadly. Lauren searched her heart and knew that deep down inside, she wanted this baby. She always wanted a child of her own. She recalled the first conversation they had about having children a few months before their wedding. Mike bluntly told her that he didn't want to be bothered with any responsibility other than himself. He admitted that he was too selfish to be a father so why bother?

Lauren loved Mike so much that she knew she didn't want to lose him. How could she sacrifice their marriage for a baby that wouldn't be wanted by the father anyway? How could she not sacrifice a living life inside of her for a man she loves dearly? Lauren could only lean on hope that maybe he would have a good reaction to the news and let her keep their baby.

Hope? Is that all she had going for her? *That's not a whole lot, but at least it's something,* she said to herself. *God, please help me make this decision wisely.* Lauren found herself sobbing at the kitchen table as she prayed. She found strength to go find her Bible. The Bible was her source of strength whenever she felt down and out about things that she couldn't figure out.

She had no family and true friends to call, so she always found comfort in prayer and reading a couple of verses to gain peace and strength.

Lauren sat down in the living room and opened the Bible. She didn't know exactly what she wanted to read. Not knowing what she was searching for, she opened to the book of Proverbs and began skimming through it. Proverbs 31 caught her eye, and she began to read. She saw herself as the woman in that chapter, the woman who worked, cooked, cleaned, took care of the house and the children. Lauren began to imagine herself as a mother raising her son and daughter to be strong and honest people who worked hard in life to get somewhere.

She imaged Mike was a strong father figure, who worked hard and disciplined the children while she spoiled them with the best clothes and most expensive toys. He would look at Lauren with adoring eyes and honor her because she would do it all. Yes, Lauren was a Proverbs woman, a strong woman who could do it all. *Mike loves me no matter what*, she convinced herself. *He will accept this pregnancy and love our baby.*

Lauren looked up and saw Mike standing in front of her. She didn't even hear the door open.

"Baby, what are you doing home so early?" Lauren asked. She was shocked to the point where she couldn't even get up off the couch.

"I had to stop home to grab some files," he replied stiffly.

Lauren nodded her head. What else could she say? She wasn't ready to tell him about the baby. *What a fine day to come home early,* she thought angrily.

"Did you clean up the carpet in the room?" Mike shouted from his work room.

"Yeah, it didn't stain." Words didn't seem to be flowing off her tongue properly. Mike came back into the living room and looked at her.

"I need you to vacuum my work room before you go to bed; it's filthy in there on the carpet. Make sure you dust it down too," Mike demanded.

Lauren became a little irritated that her husband had not asked her if she was feeling better since last night. She wanted to burst and tell him that she was pregnant. But she just knew that now was not the time to share the "good news."

"I just cleaned it two days ago, remember?" Lauren asked walking into the kitchen.

Mike did not waste time to retort angrily. "Well you didn't do a very good job."

"So … uh … what do you want for dinner today?" Lauren asked, ignoring her husbands' comment. *I am not even in the mood to argue with him right now.*

"What were you going to make?" Mike asked as he went back into the living room.

Lauren tried to sound natural and not nervous, but she knew that she wasn't doing a good job.

"Um … I was thinking about a baby roast," she answered. Luckily she caught herself. "I meant a pot roast, honey. How does that sound?" she asked.

Oh my gosh, pull yourself together! She thought nervously. A bead of sweat trickled down onto her forehead.

Mike came back into the kitchen and sat down. "Lauren, fix me a ham and cheese sandwich; you know how I like it."

She went to work on the sandwich and glanced at Mike. She studied him for a moment and decided that it wouldn't be a good idea to tell him right away. *Maybe later would be better,* she thought to herself.

"What are these?" Lauren turned around to see what Mike was talking about. The prescription bag was hanging out of her purse. Mike grabbed the bag and Lauren didn't make it to him fast enough to snatch it away. He had already snatched the bottle out of the bag and read the label on the container.

"Prenatal vitamins?" he asked. Lauren stood there in front of him, watching him read the label over and over again.

"Are *these* what I think they are?" Mike and Lauren looked at each other. She was hoping that his expression was a good type of shock and not the opposite.

Mike slammed the container of vitamins on the table. "Are you kidding me? You're *pregnant*?" Mike shouted. Her fears were confirmed; her husband was furious.

"Yes, I am pregnant, Mike. Trust me, I was just as surprised," Lauren explained. She was trying to hold back tears. She knew she had to be strong if she wanted to make some type of convincing argument about keeping the baby.

"Surprised, huh?" Mike got up from the table and paced angrily back and forth. "You planned this, didn't you?" Mike continued to shout.

"No, I didn't. I promise you I didn't, Mike. You know I take my pills every day!" Lauren couldn't fight back the tears. Mike continued to pace back and forth.

"What are you afraid of Mike? You would be a great father." She tried to be gentle and calm; she wanted nothing more than for this scene to be over with.

"No! You knew that I didn't want kids. I told you that before we got married. *You knew!*" Mike bellowed.

He rushed over to her and grabbed her by the neck and squeezed. Lauren tried to fight against his grip. She saw the rage in his eyes, the anger, and the hate. She had seen Mike angry before, but not like this. He was so angry that as he squeezed, his eyes got smaller and smaller. Suddenly, Lauren realized that it wasn't the man that she loved standing in front of her, loving her, and telling her everything was going to be okay. Instead, it was a monster practically trying to squeezing the life out of her.

"You have a choice to make," Mike sneered still holding onto her neck. "You better get rid of this baby or it's over! Make your choice soon, because I already did."

He snatched himself away from Lauren and she watched him walk out the door. She reached for her neck in pain. She couldn't believe what just took place. How could Mike put his hands on her like that? Lauren had never seen him so angry. She went to the bathroom and looked at her neck in the mirror. She could clearly see the red finger marks on her neck from where Mike pressed both his thumbs into the middle of her neck. *What am I going to do?* She thought sadly.

Lauren couldn't believe what was happening to her. Never did she dream that Mike would actually inflict pain on her body. For the first time since the doctor, Lauren placed her hand on her abdomen. Even though it was too early to feel the baby kicking, she imagined what it would be like to have little flutters inside of her from her baby. She wondered what it would be like to hold the baby in her arms and watch the smile on her husbands' face as he admired his family.

Lauren snapped out of her daydreaming when she heard her cell phone ringing in her purse. She hurried to her phone and looked at the screen, it was Mike. What could he have wanted? *Maybe he changed his mind,* she hoped. *He must be calling to apologize.* The voicemail ringer came on, and Lauren quickly dialed it back so that she could hear the message that Mike left her. He never leaves messages, so she figured that he probably felt really bad about what he did to her. Lauren listened intently to the message. There was a long pause and then a lot of rustling before Mike's voice came on the voicemail.

"I hope you made your appointment already," Lauren was not surprised at how hateful Mike sounded in the voicemail. *He really doesn't want this baby at all, or me if I decide to keep it,* she thought sadly.

The phone hung up, and Lauren was left with the choice of saving or deleting the message. She deleted it. Lauren wasn't sure what she should do or what she wanted more. She went upstairs to her room and closed the door. Abortion or marriage was her only options. As she lay in her bed, thinking and crying, she began to pray and ask God for guidance.

There was no way she could make this decision on her own. While Lauren was sobbing, she thought about her childhood without a father. She only had vague memories of her mother, who turned her over to foster care when she didn't want to be a mother anymore. The only memory of her mother was the way her hair smelled of cigarettes and her breath of liquor and vomit.

She was only six years old when her mother dropped her off at the Children and Family Services building. That was the last time she ever saw or heard of her. Lauren only admired her mother for having the decency to drop off her somewhere safe rather than leaving her on the streets to fend for herself. Having a mother was something that Lauren didn't get a chance to experience as a child, and now she desperately wanted to have that experience with her own child. Although she didn't have the proper role models of parents, Lauren knew that deep down inside, she was made to be a mother. If only she could convince Mike that he too could be a great parent.

Mike grew up with both his parents in a loving home; they were wealthy and he was spoiled. Lauren never saw Mike as a selfish man, just very spoiled and self-assured. He was well established with his own accounting firm. Mike had everything that a man would want in his life: lots of money, cars, and one of the largest, most expensive, beautiful homes on a street where mostly white people lived. *Having a child may slow him down,* she thought. *Maybe Mike would rather have me all to himself and not share me with someone else. A baby is so demanding,* she concluded. After a few hours of debating, she decided to grab the phone book to look up the number to a clinic.

Laurens' hands were shaking as she flipped through the pages. She made up her mind that this was the best decision for her to make in order for her marriage to last. How could she be so selfish to think that what she wanted was more important than what she had already agreed with from

the start? She had no right to assume that she could change anyone. Lauren had no right to believe that a baby could make someone love her more.

Tears streamed down her face again, and she quickly brushed them off. *No need to cry now*, she said to herself. *I have to do what's right for us, me and Mike. That's the way it has always been, and that is the way it should be.* Suddenly, hunger pains hit her, and she ignored them. She didn't deserve to eat or feed the unborn child in her tummy, not if she was going to kill it anyways, right?

Lauren found a clinic close to the hospital and dialed the number. To her surprise, she was shaking and her stomach was aching from being hungry.

"Thank you for calling Helping Hands Clinic for Women, how may I help you?" A woman's voice answered the phone cheerfully. For some reason, Lauren was comforted by her voice.

"Um … yes, I would like to make an appointment, please." The comfort immediately turned into nervousness again. She couldn't believe that she was going for this, that she was making an appointment to terminate the child that she wanted, the child that her husband despised and wanted nothing to do with.

"What kind of appointment ma'am?" The woman asked gently and politely. How could Lauren say the word "abortion" out loud? *Were there other awful services besides the abortions? Lauren began disgusted with the phone call and most of all with herself for even calling a clinic in the first place.*

"Well … um …" Lauren cleared her throat and tried to choose her words carefully. "I want to terminate a pregnancy." A rush of relief came over Lauren; she finally got the words out. She wanted to terminate the pregnancy for Mike, the man she loved, the man who loved her.

"Name please."

"Lauren Morgan." She took a deep breath and held it. *I cannot believe I am doing this, but I have to*, she thought sadly.

"Okay, are you more than twenty weeks pregnant?" the woman asked.

"No, I'm not," Lauren answered slowly.

She could hear the woman murmuring to herself and typing away on the computer. "I have an opening tomorrow. Is nine o'clock in the morning good for you?" Lauren could still hear her typing.

"Yes."

"Good, please be prepared to stay for a few hours after the procedure because you will not be able to drive yourself right away," she explained.

Lauren hung up the phone. It was that simple; she didn't even bother to want to know the price of the abortion or how they conducted the procedure. She didn't care to know; she was too overwhelmed with sadness. The hunger pangs began to get a little harder, followed by painful cramps. Pregnancy was something she would have taken whole-heartedly, but now this pregnancy was just a burden that she wanted nothing to do with. But at the same time, she wanted nothing more than to love her baby and take care of it. Lauren knew she would be playing with fire, especially since Mike would have nothing to do with her if she did decide to keep the baby, their baby.

Chapter Six

When Mike got home, his dinner was already hot on the table. He loosened his tie and had a seat. Lauren didn't have a chance to change and fix herself up in her dinner outfit like she usually did; she just didn't feel up to it. Mike didn't even kiss her hello or acknowledge the fact that she was in the room. She fixed her plate and sat down at the table across from him. Lauren was glad in a way that Mike wasn't talking to her. Her head felt like a hammer was pounding on her brain, and the cramps seemed to be getting worse. She knew the pains were set on by her not eating.

Lauren looked up from across her plate and noticed Mike staring at her. "What?" she asked.

"Did you make the appointment?" Mike asked sternly as he stuffed his face with a forkful of vegetables.

"Yes, I did. I have the appointment for tomorrow at nine in the morning," Lauren answered, bitterly. She picked up her glass of ice water and realized that it was still hard for her to swallow since Mike had choked her. Even swallowing the smallest pieces of food made her feel like she was swallowing a brick.

"Good." Mike grabbed the *Jet* magazine that was sitting with the mail and began to read and eat at the same time. Throughout the whole dinner, he continued to ignore Lauren as if she didn't exist. Her heart began to break slowly for herself and the baby. Tomorrow she would have to live with the fact that she was giving up something for Mike, and the least he could do was honor her and love her for that.

"Mike?" Lauren waited for him to look up at her, but all he did was grunt. "I didn't ask for this, you know. It just kinda happened." Lauren wanted to explain herself, but she didn't have too much to say along with that.

"Mike, will you please talk to me!" Lauren shouted from across the table. She quickly regretted shouting as her throat reminded her that it was still aching in the worst way that it could. She never shouted, and this time she heard her voice shaking and felt the tears pouring down her face. Mike looked more irritated than surprised that Lauren had shouted at him. He scowled at her and left her alone at the table.

Tonight, his footsteps sounded heavy as his shoes clicked and clacked on the hardwood floor. She didn't know what to do with herself. She felt like screaming and shouting and throwing the plates onto the floor. All of the excitement made her dizzy. Tonight she couldn't care less about the dishes, cleaning, or a shower. Lauren made her way to the couch and fell into a deep slumber.

Prayer did seem to come easy to her right now; she remembered what she read in Proverbs 31. She was a Proverbs woman, a woman who loved and cared for her husband, a woman who would do anything for the love of her life that she cared for deeply. A man whose last name she believed God chose for her carry. Mike chose her when no one else would. Did Mike really love her as much she thought he did? Lauren questioned her marriage for the first time.

Chapter Seven

The next morning, Lauren woke up on the couch to the sound of Mike in the kitchen rustling around. The cramps in her stomach seemed a little more intense than they were yesterday. She glanced at the time on the wall. She only had an hour and a half to get ready for her "procedure." The word sounded so horrible to Lauren in her mind, and she knew that it sounded worse when she said it out loud.

As she got up, she heard Mike grab the keys and slam the door; he was gone for the day. Relief set in, as she didn't want to deal with him today, not on the day she was going to kill her child. She touched her belly once more and knew that was the last time she would ever get to bond with her baby.

On the way to the clinic, Lauren was feeling strange pains in her abdomen and her lower back. She tried very hard ignored the pain as she assumed that she was feeling the pains because didn't eat breakfast yet. She just didn't have an appetite. There was no way food was on her mind this morning. Lauren didn't even feel up to getting dressed up in her usual dress pants or sundress. Instead she dug up a pair of gray sweat pants and a T-shirt. She believed that she didn't deserve to look her best today. Who gets dressed up to have an abortion?

The drive was long and mournful, and the cramping was going from bad to worse. *I should have at least drunk something,* she thought to herself as the pain continued to rock her body. All she could think about was Mike and how much she knew he loved her. Now he would love her even more because she was willing to make a sacrifice for him.

The last few days were awkward and harsh. He hardly spoke a word to her; it was the angriest she had seen him. Lauren wanted so desperately for things to work out between them, even if that meant ending her long-awaited pregnancy. *Oh, the things we do for love these days,* she said to herself somberly. The pains were growing more and more intense. *What is going on?* She asked herself. Parking the car, Lauren decided that it was best to sit in the car for a moment. The pains passed for about two minutes and she felt relieved. She decided to find a vending machine in the building to get something to eat before her appointment.

As Lauren walked into the building, she noticed the other women sitting in the waiting room. They looked more comfortable being there than she did. It was as if they had been there before or as if they were okay about killing their own unborn child. She slowly made her way to the secretary sitting at the desk behind the glass.

"Are you here for your appointment?" The secretary asked while she was typing on her keyboard swiftly. The woman paused for a moment and looked at her for an answer. Lauren nodded her head. *Boy, is she to the point,* she thought to herself. *Why else would I be here besides an appointment?* Lauren wanted to say out loud, meanly.

"What time is your appointment?" the receptionist asked pointedly.

"Um, nine o' clock … I think …" Lauren replied hesitantly.

"Name?" the secretary asked. Lauren was about to respond with her name when suddenly the pains in her abdomen ripped through her body as if someone was slicing her open.

"Miss?" the woman called to her. Lauren heard the woman calling her, and she realized that the women in the waiting room were gasping in horror at her. She heard a voice call for help and saw the woman behind the counter appear at her side, yelling for her to lie down and be still. The pains continued to become more intense and then Lauren realized she was screaming at the top of her lungs.

She felt the hands of the secretary laying her down and a woman in white coat yelling, "She's losing blood! She's losing blood! Call an ambulance!"

What blood? Lauren thought in between her screams. She felt her legs getting warm. Lauren refused to lie down; the pain was too much for her to bear. The woman dressed in white coat continued to try to calm Lauren down as she screamed when she saw that her gray sweats were now crimson red. The lady from behind the counter and the woman in a

white coat were talking to Lauren, asking her questions and patting the top her head with a cool cloth. The pain continued to be so unbearable that Lauren closed her eyes and waited to finish dying. Her last thoughts were of Mike and how sad he was going to be sad that she was dead.

Chapter Eight

Lauren woke up slowly. Her vision was still a little blurry, but she saw lights and heard voices that she couldn't recognize. She was exhausted and scared. *Where am I?* She wondered. Suddenly she recognized the touch of someone's hand on hers. Her eyes immediately opened; it was Mike. *How sweet, he wanted to wait for me to wake up.* Lauren turned her head toward that hand that was touching hers and saw that it wasn't Mike's. Her heart sank in disappointment; she didn't recognize the hand and became uninterested in who was there.

"I'm glad you're okay, Lauren," the voice said. Lauren heard a familiar woman's voice, gentle and concerned.

"I came as soon as I heard. How are you feeling?" The voice was Dawns'. Lauren turned her head back and looked at her face.

"I thought you were Mike," Lauren said sadly.

"Well, I called and left a message on the answering machine. Maybe he will come when he hears the message," she said gently.

"Yeah, well, I can call his office," *Lauren said. Where is Mike?* She thought irritated and impatiently.

"The hospital called his office and left a message there as soon as you got here. You feeling okay?" Dawn asked, concerned.

Lauren did appreciate Dawn's concern, but she really wanted Mike there. Tears started to well up in her eyes.

"The baby is gone, right?" Lauren asked through her tears.

Dawn nodded her head slowly.

"Yeah, you had a miscarriage, honey, at the clinic. They rushed you over in an ambulance. They found my number in your cell phone," Dawn explained gently.

Lauren was relieved that it was all over with. She just wanted to get those needles out of her arm and get back home to her husband. Just then, a nurse walked into her room. The nurse asked Dawn to excuse them, and she said goodbye to Lauren, kissed her gently on the forehead, and told her to call her if she needed anything.

The nurse walked up to Laurens' bed and pulled up a chair to sit down.

"How long do I have to be here?" Lauren asked huskily. She had cried for so long and so hard that her voice was raspy and she spoke almost as if she was whispering.

"Well, maybe until tomorrow, if we think you are well enough. You had quite an adventure today, young lady," the nurse replied. "I'm Nurse Gomez. I will be attending to you until tomorrow morning. Do you need anything to drink or a book to read?" Lauren was comforted by the nurse, since she seemed genuinely friendly and caring. She looked at the nurse and noticed that she was a lot older than she thought she was. Nurse Gomez wore a white uniform and her hair was pulled back into a tight, neat bun. Lauren guessed that she might be in her early forties.

"Do you have any children, Nurse Gomez?" Lauren found herself trying to fight tears again. She had no idea why she cared if she had children or not.

"Yes, I have two, one boy and one girl. Why do you ask?"

Lauren shrugged her shoulders in reply. *I really need to call Mike,* she thought to herself. She desperately wanted his comfort and needed him to be there with her to mourn the loss of their baby—the one that he wanted aborted.

Nurse Gomez put her hand into Lauren's and squeezed it gently. "Was this your first pregnancy?" she asked. Lauren nodded her head slowly. She didn't want to talk about it; she didn't feel like being judged or rescued from the emotions of hurt and shame.

"You know it's not the end of the world. I am sure that you can have some more one day soon," said Nurse Gomez.

Lauren then burst into tears and began to sob. Nurse Gomez was caught off guard as she looked at Lauren; she was trying her best to comfort her.

"He didn't want children! I thought maybe he would change his mind and love this one!" Lauren exclaimed while she was sobbing.

"I didn't want the abortion, but I had to do it to save my marriage! Am I a horrible person?" Lauren asked as she cried uncontrollably.

Nurse Gomez wiped away Lauren's tears with a napkin. She could relate to Lauren all too well. She was once in a marriage with a man who refused to have children, and when she ended up pregnant with her first child, he left her for another woman. Nurse Gomez never dreamed of having an abortion. She was determined to raise a child alone rather than not have one at all.

Lauren looked at the nurse with a questioning glare. "You're judging me, aren't you? I know you are. You think I'm stupid …"

"No, not stupid. I don't think you're stupid," the nurse answered carefully. Lauren was still not satisfied with her answer.

"Well, do you think I'm crazy?" Lauren asked.

Nurse Gomez squeezed Lauren's hand and looked into her eyes. "The important question is: what do you think?" Nurse Gomez stroked the top of Laurens' head.

Lauren closed her eyes. She suddenly began to picture her life as it was and what it would have been with her child and with Mike. She began to realize that the picture in her mind wasn't realistic. There was no chance, while she remained married to Mike, that she would have children. Was her dream of becoming a mother more important than her marriage? More important than Mike?

"So, what are you thinking?" Nurse Gomez asked gently.

Lauren was having a light bulb flash in her mind. It was suddenly so clear the way she saw herself and her marriage. She finally realized that she saw herself giving her life to a man who wouldn't do the same for her. Lauren realized that Mike was a man who didn't love her the way that she loved him. Lauren looked at her nurse and smiled for the first time, tears of joy due to her revelation.

"You know what? I just realized that it was time for me to take my life back."

Nurse Gomez smiled and squeezed Lauren's hand. "I was married to a man once who did all kinds of horrible things to me. He would beat me whenever I got pregnant. He didn't want children either, but I really did. I was just hoping that one day he would change his mind. I thought that if I loved him unconditionally, he would change his mind and want to have a family with me."

"Did he ever change his mind and treat you better?" Lauren asked curiously.

"No, he didn't. In fact, it got worse, not better. I did love him, but I realized that I couldn't love him more than I love myself. I needed to value myself more than him. I prayed to God every night to give me the strength to leave him, because I was afraid to love anyone else," Nurse Gomez explained. "I did get pregnant and when I refused to have an abortion he kicked me and pregnant belly out of his house and his life." Lauren admired the way Nurse Gomez told her story without crying or seeming over emotional about her past. *I guess one day I will get over my miscarriage.* Lauren thought sadly as she brushed a tear off her cheek.

"I didn't have an education or a job at the time I left my husband so I had no way to support myself or my son. I finally went to school for nursing and got a job here after I graduated. Everything also seemed to fall together perfectly when I decided to turn my life over to God."

Lauren admired her story. How would her story end? *God I know I need you now more than ever,* Lauren prayed to herself.

She wondered if she had the guts to leave Mike. He was the man who took her in and provided for her. How in the world could she leave that behind?

"Don't worry yourself too much," the nurse said. "Put everything in the hands of God and things will work out for you." The nurse put it so simply that Lauren wished there was more to it.

She began to replay their marriage in her mind. Had she put God first in her life? She had to be honest with herself and admit that Mike was the center of her world, so much that she put him before God and herself. It was a hard pill to swallow, but Lauren worshipped her husband instead of God.

"I realize that Mike has been my god for years now. I have been practically living up my husbands' standards and following his commandments. I wish I could have seen this sooner," Lauren said. "The sad thing is that I was in the clinic having the abortion for him. I wanted to keep the baby, but I decided that I didn't want to keep it at the expense of my marriage. Instead of going through with the abortion, I ended up having a miscarriage right there at the clinic. Isn't that the craziest thing?"

"Honestly, no it isn't," the nurse answered. "Sometimes things have to happen in order for us to start somewhere and get somewhere. Believe me, this is your stepping stone right here, right now. It's just up to you what you're gonna do."

The sudden realization of her life and what it was startled Lauren, but she was grateful that someone could relate to her and understand her without judging her. Now all she had to do was figure out where to go from here. Was she ready to leave Mike? Could she leave him? *Maybe he will change to be the man I know he can be,* she thought to herself hopefully.

Lauren began to think about the ways that Mike treated her, all the good things, but there weren't that many. He did provide her a home, a car, nice designer clothes, and money when she needed it. She never needed to work or find a job. The only thing that Lauren wished she had more of in her marriage was actually the love she wanted from Mike, the security in knowing that he loved her and cared for her. *Does Mike love me?* She wondered sadly.

After searching deep down in her heart, she knew the truth. She knew it all along. Mike didn't love her; she was his little trophy, his maid, a warm body at night (if he ever touched her), and his only security that he was a man because he was able to control her. Lauren sighed deeply and thought angrily to herself: *If he really loved me, he would be here and he would have at least called to check on me.* Lauren realized that she was growing angry and disgusted with Mike. She knew what she had to do, and it would be painful. It was time for her to think like a Proverbs woman, it was time to grow up and stand up.

Lauren wiped her eyes and sat up on the bed.

"You know what, nurse?" Lauren whispered as if she was telling a secret.

"What?" Nurse Gomez gazed at her, waiting for her to speak.

"I just realized that I was in love with potential all along. It's time for me to take a stand on my life. I'm ready to take it back," she said slowly.

"Well, I wish you good luck with whatever decisions you make. It sounds like you have your mind made up. Just remember to keep God first in everything that you do and he will see you through. I promise you, he will not lead you astray." Nurse Gomez gave Lauren a hug and walked toward the door.

Chapter Nine

Lauren was relieved that Mike wasn't home. Although he hadn't even called or visited her while she was in the hospital, she decided that she wasn't going to hold any malice in her heart about it. Instead, she prayed long and hard. She asked for forgiveness and decided that today was the day she was going to start over and build a relationship with God.

The first place she went when she got home was her closet. She found an old suitcase and quickly filled it up with her shoes and her clothes. She made her way quickly to the dresser and threw in her undergarments, perfumes, and lotions. Despite the soreness she was still feeling in her abdomen, Lauren moved quickly, determined to not meet up with her soon-to-be ex-husband.

"What are you doing?" A voice behind boomed loudly. Lauren turned around quickly and saw Mike standing at the doorway with a bouquet of flowers. *Flowers? What is he doing? Why is he home so early?* A million questions continued to race through her mind as she saw him standing there in his beige work suit. He had a confused look on his face until he noticed the suitcase filled with clothes.

"Are you going somewhere?" Mike asked coolly.

Lauren wanted to stand her ground, no matter what he said or did. She didn't want to talk or say too much. She nodded her head and continued to pack. There wasn't too much left to say.

"Is that your cab downstairs?" Mike asked.

"Yeah Mike it is," Lauren answered calmly.

Mike went over to Lauren and looked at her. She could tell that he was trying not to sound angry.

"Do you want to tell me what exactly is going on right now?" he asked walking closer to her.

Lauren took a deep breath and chose her words carefully. "I'm divorcing you, Mike."

Lauren didn't bother to look at his face when she delivered the news. She noticed that he was still holding the bouquet of red roses.

"Are those for me?" Lauren asked as she closed her suitcase.

"Yeah, I went by the hospital, and they told me you had gone home," he answered. He spoke slowly as if he were trying to digest the news. Lauren was not impressed with his "effort" of trying to be there for her. He had more than twenty-four hours to be concerned about his wife.

"Well, I was there all day yesterday. You didn't call me or come to see me." Lauren was pushing back the tears; she refused to let him see her cry.

"Look, I know I wasn't there, and I have no excuse. I bought you these roses hoping you would still be there. I am sorry for being so horrible to you." Mike reached over and touched Lauren on her cheek tenderly.

Lauren made the tragic mistake of looking in his eyes as he spoke to her. He sounded so genuine and sincere as he pronounced every word with the upmost love and care. Lauren began to see the man she fell in love with, the man she desired to spend the rest of her life with.

"I feel bad about everything. You do so much ... I guess ... I was afraid ..." Mike put the flowers on the dresser and took a seat on the bed with his hands over his face. Lauren could have sworn she heard him sobbing. *Is this for real?* Lauren asked herself. *Is this man really crying?*

She watched him as he sat there sobbing. A tear fell from his hand onto his jacket. Lauren was suddenly taken aback from all the emotion that she wasn't prepared for. The love for Mike had returned, the sincerity she felt for him returned, but she knew down inside there was no hope for her if she stayed with him for rest of her life.

At least that's what she thought, until Mike said the magic words: "I want a child with you, Lauren. You're my wife, and we should be building a family together." Mike looked up from his hands and dried his face with the sleeve of his coat. Lauren never thought she would ever hear those words. Everything she needed to hear was suddenly being said. *A family?* Lauren thought. *Wow, is this really happening?* She wasn't prepared for this moment, and was at a loss for words.

"You want a family with me, Mike?" Lauren asked.

"Yeah, I do, I missed this opportunity, and because of me, we lost it. I want a baby with you, I really do. Let's do this for real this time. I never thought I would ever want to be a father, but now I know I do. I just couldn't face it with you … because … I was a coward."

Mike continued, "You're a good woman, and I take you for granted. You cook for me, clean; your love for me is real. All I do is ignore and hurt you. I'm so sorry for treating you less than you deserve. You deserve the world, and I want to give it to you. I want a chance to make things right."

Mike stood up and walked over to Lauren. He took her by the hand and leaned down and kissed her softly. The last time he kissed her like that was on their wedding day. She began to think that this must be a sign that things could be better for them, that Mike finally wanted to treat her like the Proverbs woman she was. She did love him very much, and now he was finally willing to be a better man, a better husband.

Chapter Ten

Their tender moment was interrupted by the cab driver honking the horn. She remembered that she hadn't paid the driver and he was waiting for her. Lauren dreamed of this moment and didn't want to throw it all away. Mike looked her as she looked at the cab through the window. She could tell that Mike was waiting to see if she was really leaving. His eyes began to plead with her. The horn blew again impatiently.

"Would you like for me to go down to the cab?" Mike asked.

Lauren imagined that if she was to stay with Mike, they would have a happy home, loving each other and their children unconditionally. She began to see herself as a wife and soon-to-be mother again. The dream that she sought after since was a little girl playing house was finally coming true, and there was no way that she could miss this opportunity. Why should she? Everyone deserves love and happiness, right?

"Yes, Mike, could you please go down to the cab?" Lauren requested gently. This was it, her moment of truth. Her dreams seemed distant at first, but now they were finally coming true. She kissed Mike again and looked into his big brown eyes and smiled. She didn't want this moment to pass her by.

Mike grinned at her and headed for the door to go downstairs.

Lauren called after him, "Could you please apologize to the driver for me and tell him I will be right down?"

Mike stopped in his tracks and looked at Lauren, confused. "I don't understand. I thought you weren't leaving."

"No, Mike, I am leaving. It's time for me to live my own life now. There is no guarantee that things will get better or that you will treat me

any better. I have to leave and go on my own," Lauren explained. "You're just too late, Mike."

Lauren grabbed her suitcase and began wheeling it out the door. Mike continued to stand frozen at the doorway as he watched Lauren walk out of the bedroom they once shared. He watched Lauren through the window as she got into the back seat of the cab and saw the driver put the suitcase into the trunk.

Epilogue—Lauren's Journal

It has been almost a year since I saw Mike. I have to admit that sometimes I miss him. The road to starting over wasn't necessarily easy, but I managed to get through it. Thankfully, the divorce is finally over and Mike even offered to give me alimony, but I reluctantly declined the offer! I just wanted to sever all ties with him completely. I wasn't after his money in the first place; I just wanted to be free of him for good.

It took awhile for me to forgive him and then to forgive myself, but I made up my mind that I didn't want him to have power over my emotions, even while I am not with him. Sometimes I wonder what I would be doing right now if I had decided to trust Mike and stay with him. I have to admit, it feels good to wake up in my own apartment, make my own breakfast if I feel like it, and skip cooking dinner if I don't want to.

I have a freedom that I hadn't felt while I was married. I love my life. I have a good job as a teacher assistant at the middle school, and I am finally going back to school for my teaching degree. I learned that I can do all things through Christ that gives me the strength and abilities to do all things.

I may not understand it all right now, but I do know that I serve God first and not man. I have a peace, joy, and strength that I never felt before I turned my life over to Him. Now, I'm ready to go through anything, only because I know that if God can bring me to it, He will bring me through it!

Love, Power, and a Sound Mind

This section of the book was written to encourage you that your trials are the building blocks for your future. Everything that you are going through has to work out for your good (Romans 8:28).

Can You Hear Me?

Lord, I know You hear me.
I am crying out to You.
I hold on to You even when I feel like letting go.
How many nights do I have to cry out?
How many pillows must I soak at night?

Lord, I know You hear me.
I cry out in pain.
I feel like I'm going insane.
But I can't lose my mind today,
    that can't be what You have for me.

I know Your plans for me are bigger
    than my own eyes can see.
Won't You lead me?
Won't You show me the way?
Lord, I know You hear me.

You answered me, Lord,
    in that sweet voice of Yours.
I hear Your answers through my anger,
    but my pride consumes me.

Please, Lord, I hear You now,
    forgive me for my pride.
Thank You for drying my pillows tonight.

Tonight, I can rest peacefully,
    because I know that You heard me.

Lord, I know that You can hear me.

I used to think to myself that I was the greatest sinner there was. Although no sin is greater than any other sin, the way I was living my life led me to believe in my mind that I was "unsaveable." That is how I was feeling about myself, and the devil confirmed it in my mind that God didn't really want to have anything to do with me because I was too far deep into a lifestyle that God was not pleased with.

The truth is that God loved me, even as a sinner. After living many years running from God, I finally ran into Him. I rededicated my life to Him, and I have been in a relationship with Him since then. God called me out of my darkness and into a new light that has never been brighter.

He brought me out of my sin, to bring me in closer to Him. He quickly revealed the purpose that He placed on the inside of me before I was even born. I thank Him every day for calling me out of my sinful life of drugs, fornication, alcohol, and thoughts of suicide. I am still a work in progress but thank God for being a redeemer when I do slip and fall. The Bible says in Psalms 80:3, "O God, restore us and cause your face to shine upon us, and we will be saved (NAS version)."

God chose me before I was born to be His daughter. Romans 8:31 says: "If God is for us, who can be against us?" The Bible also says in Romans 8:37–39, that nothing can separate us from the love of God. No matter what the sins are.

Don't be discouraged when you feel like you're not worthy of the love of God. The truth is that we don't deserve it. The good news is that He loves us anyway.

Wanna Be Close to You

I wanna be close to You.
I want to be in love with You.
I want to know Your love and strength.
In Your love and strength,
I will have power and strength
    in me.

I am delivered from depression,
condemnation, and self-annihilation,
    'cause I'm closer to You.

I wanna be where Your love is.
I wanna see my destiny
    and what You have for me.
I only wanna be close to You.

Without a spirit of fear;
But with spirits of love,
    power, and a sound mind.
I will be closer to You,
'Cause I have the desire to be close to You.

When I was younger, my friends would always tell me: "Try this! Try that! Go here! Do this!" My friends never told me to jump off a cliff, thank God! My point is this: "Try God!" It is that simple. Try Him. He is awesome. He is great. He can do anything, even the impossible. Yes, the impossible! What can God do for you today? The answer is simple: anything!

The things that God has allowed me to go through with love, drugs, and trying to commit suicide multiple times has led me to where I am today. It is easy to talk about the things I have been through in my life because I am delivered from my past. I am glad to say that I have been delivered from my mess.

The best thing that ever happened to me, besides the birth of my children, was experiencing the power of God. Experiencing God is something that I am willing to participate in for the rest of my life. I am excited about the things that God has for me, and I am excited about what He has in store for you. Like myself, you're still a *great* work in the making; don't give up when you mess up! Give in! Let God restore, redeem, and replenish you with His strength and unconditional love. You don't need to try to fix yourself, let God do it for you. Let Him into your life!

The best part about experiencing God is realizing and recognizing the love that He has for you. 1 Corinthians 13:8 says it simply: "Love never fails." From "experience" I know that to be true. I thank God every day that I have the power of love, peace, and a sound mind (2 Timothy 1:7).

All of It

I give You all the glory.
I give You all the praise.
'Cause You and only You
    were there to see me through.

I give You all the praise because
You allowed me to see another day
    to raise my hands to You and give
    You the highest praise.

I call You "Holy" because there is
    no other holier than You,
For if there was, I would call out
    their name, O Lord.
But as for me, I know only You.

To You I give honor because You
    have always seen me through.
For You I lift up heaven just to be
Close to You.

I magnify Your name because if it
    wasn't for you, God, I would be
Dead in my sin.

But because of You, O Lord,
    I'm reborn again.
I can live again, thank you Lord.
I give You all the praise.
To only You will I continue

To sing Your praises.
I give You all the glory.
All the praise.
I give You all of it.

1 Corinthians 1:9 says: "God is faithful." I really don't have to embellish on that except to say that He is faithful. Psalms 92 says that it is good to declare God's love and kindness in the morning and His faithfulness at night (v. 2).

God has been so good to me. I can sing of His grace, mercy, and favor all day. Psalms 50:15 says, "Call upon me in your day of trouble and I shall rescue you, and you will honor me (NAS version)." How great is our God?

Think about the last time God rescued you from death, sickness, anger, oppression, your dangerous mate, drugs, financial woes, and even the time He rescued you from yourself. When I think about the times He has rescued me, I feel like saying "thank you" is simply not enough. God is so good that He is better to us than we are to ourselves. Begin to thank God and praise Him for who He is, what He has already done, and what He is about to do in your life.

Where I Wanna Be

Where Lord? Where are You?
I told You that I wanted to be over here.
I prayed for this the last time.
You told me to have faith.
But where are You now?

I am over here.
Is this not where You wanted me to be?
The place where I have been praying to be?

I just don't get it, I don't understand.
You told me to have faith.
Here is my faith, and here is where I am.
I beckon You to come, Lord.
Show up where I am.
Please, I beg You!

I don't know where I went wrong.
Please come and rescue me!
Remove me from where I am.

Okay, Lord, I'm moving.
Where do You want me to be?
I see, over there.
That's where you want me to be.
Over there with You.
Where You are is where I want to be.

You were waiting for me all this time to find You.
And right here is where I wanna be.
Wherever you are.

There was a point in my life when I was ready to move from the little town in Georgia where I was living. I was ready for big things and a new life for my daughter in Virginia. I prayed to God for the longest time for a job. Suddenly job interviews were coming up and doors seemed to be opening up for me. It seemed like the right time for me to move on to bigger and better things. Although I seemed hopeful and I believed in God for a job and a place to live; I did eventually get a job. The funny thing is that while I was at this job, it didn't feel right to me.

I began to feel like I didn't belong there, it felt like I was out of place. I was also unable to get an apartment, because I had bad credit. I continued to work for a few days until I decided to move back to Georgia. Thank God I didn't give up my apartment in Georgia! I went back to my apartment defeated and sad about the fact that I didn't get to move.

I was living in a roach-infested one-bedroom apartment. I began to understand that I was still in Georgia for a reason. I had no idea why I was still in Georgia, but I felt at peace about the situation instead of anxious. I told God one day: "God, I know that I am supposed to be here now, and I understand that, but I need a new place to live." I told God what kind of apartment I wanted, I told Him exactly what I needed, and He did for me above and beyond what I was even asking for.

I believe God has kept me in Georgia for a reason. I am not sure exactly what that reason is, but I am trusting Him to reveal that to me in due time. Until then, my goal is to continue to live the purpose that God has placed inside me. The Bible says in Proverbs 16:1 that we can plan our paths, but ultimately God has the final say-so on what we will do or where we will go in life.

I always keep God in the back of my mind when I am making decisions, because I want Him to be included in my life. Are you making plans and making decisions without God's final say-so? Pray about things before you make a decision and believe that God is in control and that He will direct your paths always.

This Is the Day

Today I praise You.
For this day I worship You.
Because You love me.
Even when I don't love myself.
Even when I felt like giving up.
I'm pressing in, O Lord.
I want to be closer to You today.
I can honestly say that I love You today.
I need You on this day and everyday.
Everyday I need you more and more.
There is nothing that I can do today without You.
I worship you today.
You're my only Lord and God today.
No one else completes me.
No one else matter to me but you, on this day.
This is the day that I vow to worship and honor you.
This is the day.

When I think about my past, I thank God for loving me more than I loved myself. I believe that because of His love, I am alive today. I give God all the honor and all the glory, because He didn't have to save me. He could have left me for dead. God chose me to go through those trials because He knew that I would make it.

Are you going through emotional turmoil right now and you don't know how you will make it? Just think that God is taking you through those trials and tribulations so that He will get the glory in the end. His glory is greater than the suffering that you are going through. The Bible says in Romans 5:3 that tribulations bring about perseverance. When God is able to work things out in our favor, we can't help but give Him thanks and glory, because no one else but God could do it for us.

For example, in my own experience, there was a time when I had no money in the bank and the rent was due in a couple days. I wasn't working at the time, and I was about eight months pregnant with my daughter. I heard a voice in my head say: "Go check your savings account." I was thinking to myself: "What for? I don't have any money in there." I checked my account and there was almost four hundred dollars in there! That was enough to pay my rent and the light bill!

Ever since that day, anytime I got into a situation where it looked like something was about to get turned off, I just began to praise God and believe that He work it out somehow. He has never disappointed me! The Bible says in Romans 8:25 that if we hope for what we cannot see, with perseverance we should wait for it. When we need something or when we are expecting something supernatural to happen, we should definitely seek Him for it and wait patiently for it, because He is always on time. Take a moment to just love on God in your own special way; tell Him how great He has been to you and how much you love Him. Remember that praise is your weapon. When you begin to praise God, no matter the situation, He will move on your behalf.

See Another Day

Thank you, Lord, for taking me from where I was.
You allowed me to see to live and see this day.
I'm not perfect.
At least I'm not where I used to be.
Where You are taking me tomorrow, I cannot fathom.
I'm so glad that You called me out of darkness.
You rescued me from my foolish ways.
I don't know where I would be today if it wasn't for You.
I should be dead and gone by now, but You kept me.
For that I am thankful.
You allowed me to see another day.

When I was a young woman, there was a time when the enemy was trying to take me out. I almost let him. I remember a time when I was sitting in the dark by myself, crying out. I was thinking to myself that I had no purpose here on earth. I thought to myself that I could punish the people who hurt me by killing myself. Killing myself would allow the people who hurt me to feel the way that I was feeling: hurt, guilt, shame, and defeat. Of course, I was being selfish, because if I killed myself, I would be hurting my family, my "real friends", and especially my sisters. Unfortunately, at that particular time, I didn't care who I hurt.

I convinced myself that they would get over it because they are stronger than me emotionally anyway. I went to the nearest store and bought the largest size of Nyquil, one bottle of extra-strength Tylenol, one bottle of extra-strength Advil, and a large bottle of aspirin. I went to the car and I swallowed every last pill and flushed them down with the Nyquil. I sat in my car, waiting for the euphoria of death to sink in. I grew impatient and I was thinking to myself: "Why am I not dead yet?" I couldn't figure out why I was feeling just fine. The combination of the medicines did nothing for me. I grew angry and drove off to my friend's house. As I was driving, I felt a little woozy but nothing happened.

When I got to my friend's house, I told her what I had done. I was rushed to the hospital. As soon as I got there, they were doing tests and poking me with stuff. A doctor came in the room and showed me a chart and told me that I should be in a coma or dead due to the amount of medicine I had taken. I didn't understand then, but while I was helping the enemy to take me out, but God was keeping me for a reason.

Are you feeling invisible in life? Do you feel like you don't matter? Just remember that God can see you and that He thinks that you matter. He is calling on you today to trust in who He is and what the Word says about you. Trust and believe that He will see you through the tunnel. He will walk with you until you reach the end of the tunnel, where the light is.

Who You Are

The desires of my heart, You will give me.
The understanding that I need, You will give me.
The wisdom that I want, I must ask for.
The way in which I am to walk, won't be easy.
The shoulder that I need, is Yours, Lord.
The friend that I want, I can find in You.
The answers that I need, I can seek You for them in Your word.
The strength that I don't have, You will give me.
I can find You in prayer, Father.
You are my everything.
The everything that I need, now and forevermore.
You are faithful, trustworthy, that's who you are.

Ever since I have rededicated my life to God, He has poured endless blessings into my life. To me, it's not really all about what God can do for me, it is about who He is. God has used me, on occasion, to be a blessing to other people, but the best part about watching God do a work in other people's lives is watching the change that people have when they encounter Him and His goodness.

The more I seek God, more of my desires are fulfilled, according to His purpose, of course. The Bible says in Psalms 37:4, "Delight yourself in the Lord, and He will give you the desires of your heart (NAS version)." The walk with God isn't an easy one, because you have to give up things that you are used to.

When I started my walk with God, I had to delete a lot of contacts out of my phone. I had to give up my Lil Wayne fetish (I'm still a work in progress with that), along with the drugs, excessive drinking, and the clubbing. Since I started my walk with God, I have gained so much wisdom, knowledge, and understanding about life and how to handle life trials and tribulations when things come up that I cannot control.

Do not lean on your own understanding as the Bible says, but instead ask for wisdom, and God will give it to you (James 1:5). Sometimes the walk gets a little rough and you will feel like throwing in the towel, but if you stay in God's corner and fight with Him, your life will have its greatest wishes and desires fulfilled according to His will in a supernatural way. Stick with God and run after His heart. Have a relationship with Him, don't practice religion with Him.

Lord, if You Want To

Lord, if You want to, You change things right now.
Lord, if You want to, You will show me the way.
Guide me today, Father.
Show me what to do; I am lost right now, Father.
I don't know what to do.
Where should I go?
What should I do?
Why me?
Why now?
These are the questions that I have.
I need you, Lord.
Right now, today.
Father, I know I cannot see what it is You have for me.
No, not now; no, not yet.
Father, I will wait for You.
To show me the way.
Because I know that You're always on time.
It is Your will, Lord, not mine.
Lord, I know if You want to, I'll never be left behind.
Lord, if You want to, I know you will take me through.

How faithful is He? The man who loves us and cares for us. God is faithful, He is wonderful, and He is great. I could go on and on about how marvelous He is. I believe God for all things. I believe Him for healing, finances, deliverance, guidance, and wisdom among many other things. I don't believe in always seeking God's hand, but I believe in seeking His face. I live to watch His glory manifest not only in my life, but other people's lives. The next time you see something that seems impossible to be resolved, just think to yourself or out loud that if God wants to right then, He could turn this situation around. For example, if you're in your car one morning and it doesn't want to start, just say: "Lord, if You want to, You can start my car right now!" Wait and watch Him do it with anything in your life. The Bible says to be anxious for nothing but wait patiently for everything.

Made in the USA
Lexington, KY
22 May 2017

SOMETHING WORTH LIVING FOR

H.T. STEPHENS

Mel,

Thank you for giving me the courage to go after what I want. I hope you enjoy my words.

♡ *H.T. Stephens*